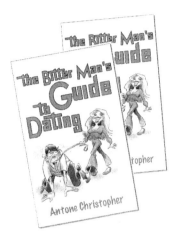

Antone Christopher
The Bitter Man

For a copy of my book
visit me at:
www.thebitterman.us
thebitterman@earthlink.net

The Bitter Man's GUIDE TO DATING

www.thebitterman.us

by **Antone Christopher**
aka "The Bitter Man"

Illustrations by Jeff Mandell
www.caricature.com

Copyright © 2004 by Antone Christopher

Published by The Bitter Man Publications
Orlando, Florida

Associated logos are trademarks and/or registered trademarks of
The Bitter Man Publications

Printed in the United States of America

The Bitter Man Publications 2004

This book is dedicated in loving memory to my
Mother and Father
Sister - Angela
Brother - Alfred
You are now my guardian angels

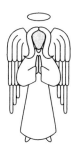

You spend your life looking for the right babe,
but everyone you meet has a default in their being,
in their head and in their soul.
I can't believe whats happening.
I've given up on my chance to meet the
girl of my dreams, a girl to romance.
I gave them all I can.
That's why I'm the Bitter Man.

ALZO

Special Thanks

I wish to thank my wonderful family and friends who supported and encouraged me to continue my "Bitter Quest."

Viktoria - Thank you for your positiveness and always making me happy. You are truly sweet and . . .

Zahide - Thank you for your spiritual support, love and friendship.

Debbie Marcet - Thank you for your time spent with me working on your computer late at night and making this book come to life.

Jeff Mandell - Thank you for your incredible cartoons. You are truly a gifted artist.

Tony Firriolo - Thanks for driving down to the Miami Book Fair with me and being the best friend anyone could have.

Rick Fernandez - Thanks for being an angel to me.

Alana Corcella - Thanks for your sisterly love and funny conversations that keep me alive.

I Thank all the girls who treated me with disrespect and never took the time to get to know and appreciate who I truly am.

Foreward

by the author

Hi my name is Antone Christopher. Thanks for reading my book. Before you begin, I'd like to tell you a little about myself, and what you're about to read.

First let me tell you about who I am. I was born in Manhattan, NY, and was raised in the suburb of Stony Brook, Long Island. I came from a very artistic, musical, and dance-oriented family. It was a family filled with love and good values.

Ever since first grade, I can remember being attracted to girls, I always wanted to have a girlfriend and romance. Even in grade school, junior high, and high school, I set out to capture the attention of my heart's desire. But my efforts were to no avail. I was friendly, not bad looking and I always tried to be the nice guy and talk to the girls I was attracted to. But nothing developed beyond casual friendships. As the years went on, I still pursued women, asking them out whenever possible in hopes that I would find that special someone. Oh yeah, I had the occasional date or fling, but nothing serious. I began to get frustrated during my high school and college years, thinking to myself It'll happen soon, I'm still young enough.

I had been studying music in college to become a musician and I thought if I got into a good band, surely I could get a girlfriend. But still, it didn't happen. It was something I had really wanted since junior high school. Finally, when I was in my mid-twenties, I met an exchange student from Germany. We dated and fell in youthful love. It was great and I was so happy! We dated for two years and then got married. It then became a seven-year rocky road. Needless to say, it wasn't a match made in heaven. But we loved each other and tried very hard to work things out. Unfortunately, it didn't work out and we got divorced. But we have remained good friends to this day.

Looking for a fresh start on life, I packed up in the cold of a New York winter and headed for the warmth of Florida, the Sunshine State, where I now reside.

After my divorce and dealing with the aftermath and healing, I began searching for someone special once again - just like many of you are doing. Thus began my decade of dating. I've always had the highest regard for women, and still do. But after dating many women over the past 10 years and being used and rejected by most of them, my views began to change. Now you can read and learn from my experiences and find out why my book is called "The Bitter Man's Guide to Dating."

One of the most important reasons I've written this book is to have people realize that no matter how many books have been written on the "bad guys" and "trashing men" (and they're in the hundreds), there are just as many bad girls out there. I can't believe how many books and talk shows discuss nasty guys and men are jerks, etc., etc. Don't get me wrong, I'm aware of the notorious bad boys out there. But what about the good guys? And there are plenty of us. Why do we have to take the rap for the bad guys? When we're on a date, the good guys are trying to be gentlemen and treat a woman right. But most women are not interested in the nice guys, and they go right back to dating the jerks. They blame ALL of the guys for their problems, when it's often their fault for dating guys like this in the first place. Thus begins the cycle of women vs. man and vice versa. So how about most women, are they all perfect? Do you think it's possible there might be one or two out there that are abusive, unfaithful, insensitive, self-centered, controlling, or possibly just a plain old witch? I think it's possible! In fact, if you search through my Character Definitions, you might just learn how to avoid a girl that could potentially make you a **BITTER MAN**.

BITTER CONTENTS

Character Definitions

All of the character definitions in this section are based on women I've met in my dating life. While reading this, keep in mind that one woman may possess qualities of more than one definition. For example, you might find a combination "Pet Owner Obsessor / Mystery Woman" or a "Career Searcher / Uptight Chick." If you can identify one or more of these characteristics in your date, it doesn't necessarily mean she's an inherently bad person. My intent here is to share with you some of the female personality types I've run across in my dating life, in hopes that it will help you to be aware of, and avoid character traits that don't compliment your personality or lifestyle. Thus avoiding relationship conflict.

- Note -

* CDs = Character Definitions

* Note: Let us not forget that most of these CDs can be found in male personalities as well.

Attitude Chicks

Watch out for this kind of chick. Observe this type of chick from afar — because that's where you want her to stay. This type of girl will only open up and be friendly to someone she feels can benefit her in some way. She may be cordial, but will generally be cold in her attitude towards anyone she feels doesn't benefit her. Attitude chicks are often physically attractive. But don't be taken by their physical beauty, Attitude Chicks can appear attractive on the outside, but on the inside they can be ugly and shallow. If she is friendly to some and unfriendly to others, this is not a sign of a healthy person. Some of the CDs she might associate with are _Negative Smokers, Bull$#itter Chicks, Cell Phone Chicks, High Maintenance women, Users, Hair Flippers / Mirror Lookers,_ and _Gold Diggers._ So my advise is don't give this chick the time of day. She is not worth it! And you can bet your bottom dollar that if you date an attitude chick, her attitude will become your problem real soon.

Automobile Door Unlockers

Automobile Door Unlockers are some of the nicest dates to be on. This is a girl who will get in the passenger seat and then reach over to the driver's side or press the button to unlock the door for you. These types of girls are often caring people who are positive and fun to be with. That's a good thing! She has the potential to be a great date. Enjoy!

Baggage Babes

Baggage Babes are the types of women that have all kinds of past and present problems. The majority of these problematic females are generally 30 years old and up. Why? Because that's the age they usually start collecting their piles of luggage. Some of the topics a Baggage Babe will discuss are as follows:

* Her Ex Husband or Ex Boyfriend treats her with disrespect
* Her children have no respect for anything or anyone
* She's in therapy
* She hates men
* She's thinking of becoming a lesbian
* She wants a new start in life but doesn't know where to begin

Baggage Babes are often cynical and skeptical of men in general. They carry their mental, emotional and financial problems everywhere and want to drop their baggage at your front door. My advice is to keep your door locked!

Bartender Babes

Here's a chick that's a tough cork to pop! Bartender chicks are often macho/strong minded party girls that have a serious attitude if you rub them the wrong way. These tough outer shell girls have heard all the pick up lines and deal with all types of people from normal to crazy to drunk slobs! Thus often giving them their callous exterior. So if you're interested in asking a bartender chick out on a date, the way I suggest is to go to her bar frequently and try to get a casual conversation going . . . possibly about the latest fad type of drink or comment on her tattoo. But don't expect too much attention WHY?? Because bartender chicks have so many guys constantly hitting on them and checking them out, it would take something different for them to be truly attracted to a customer. But if you're a good looking, cool, macho dude that's quick with a joke and lights up her smoke, you may just make this bartender's heart tender. Oh yeah and don't forget to leave her a big tip!

Boozer Babes

I guess I have to write about this type of chick because everyone says "You need to write about chicks that get trashed." So by popular demand, this is what I've learned about Boozers. These are the types of girls who drink like a fish, and I'm not talking about soft drinks. You see and meet them at parties and bars. They range from young to old, and shy to bold. And of course, there are different levels of boozers, from casual to obsessive. But the kind I'm talking about are the obsessive boozers that keep on drinking until they get hammered. They don't seem to have any self-control or know what their limit is. They also don't seem to care if they drink excessively, get sick, puke or embarrass themselves. I definitely sense serious mental issues, and I wouldn't touch a boozer with a case of Jack

Daniels. But if you're a boozer guy and enjoy hanging out at bars and hitting the bottle, then may I suggest you attend a local AA meeting and you may just hook up with the Boozer Babe of your dreams. But if you're a semi-normal guy and not sure how to spot a boozer, let me give you a few clues to look for:

If you're in a social drinking situation, observe:

✳ What she's drinking and approximately how many she's been slamming down. If it's more than 3 or 4 drinks within a 2 hour period, then this could be a **possible** red flag observance.

✳ If she's getting sloppy, loose, stumbling, slurring her speech, tripping, knocking things over, speaking loudly, saying stupid things and getting obnoxious in any way, these are all signs of a boozer who can't handle her alcohol, and this is a **definite** red flag observance.

✳ If she appears to be in her own little world, **quietly** getting intoxicated with one drink after the next until she passes out on the sofa, bed, floor, chair or closet etc. this could be the sign of a serious silent boozer. She needs help! This is a **major** red flag.

✳ If she's approximately between the ages of 18-23 and she's drinking lots of beer at a sports bar, frat party, pool party, etc. then the chances are she's just experiencing the "Let's get drunk and party" stage of her life. She'll most likely grow out of it.

✳ If she's getting drunk and horny (this is most guy's dream come true), then you now have been faced with the one most difficult decisions ever known to mankind (to do or not to do, this is the question). But if she's a true horny boozer, this could be common practice for her, so **beware!** Boozer Babes will often associate with <u>Attitude Chicks</u>, <u>Messy Car Girls</u>, <u>Negative Gum Chewers</u>, <u>Problem Girls</u>, <u>Opinionators</u>, <u>Trashy Chicks</u>, <u>and Negative Smokers</u>.

So don't get discouraged if you hook up with a boozer, just think: not only can you take her on a cheap date to a local bar on Thursday night when ladies drink free, but you can always count on plenty of sloppy drunk sex, a stocked liquor cabinet, mental baggage and a screwed-up life . . . bottoms up!

BOOZER BABES

Bull$#itter Chicks

Bull$#itter (BS) chicks are similar to bull$#itter guys. They feel they have to impress you by informing you of all the power, knowledge, and experience they **think** they have. BS chicks want to impress you because they are generally insecure and this is how they make themselves feel important. Some examples of BS lines they might feed you are:

* ✸ "I can get you a job there, I'm friends with the owner"
* ✸ "I used to own a Mercedes"
* ✸ "I was partying in LA last weekend"
* ✸ "My best friend owns a condo on the beach"
* ✸ "I can get us a free limo for the weekend"
* ✸ "I've been there, done that"
* ✸ "I can get us back stage"
* ✸ "I can get us free drinks, I know the bartender"
* ✸ "Let me make a few phone calls"

BS girls can be a real problem, and you may not get along with them because you never know if you can take them seriously. But they do get along well with BS guys. Wow! When these two get together, you'll need a net to catch the bull$#it that's flying! The only problem with these types of girls is they usually don't last long in relationships and will need a new boyfriend approximately every few months. Why is that you ask? Because that's about how long it takes the average guy to see through the BS lines he's been eating for the past few months. BS girls usually smoke and like to frequent nightclubs where they can BS to their peers. Some of the personality types these girls like to socialize with are _Attitude Chicks_, _Smokers_, _Negative Gum Chewers_, _Problem Girls_, _Gold Diggers_, _Boozer Babes_, _Trashy Chicks_ and _Opinionators_. So if you're a BS Guy, then it's a match made in BS heaven!

Busy Bee / Goal Getters

Busy Bees are everywhere these days - both men and women. You must be careful when dating these kinds of women. They tend to have their schedules so busy with work, friends, family, working out and their career goals that you tend to wonder, if I get involved with someone like this, would they have time for me? Where would I fit in? Would we have quality time together? Chances are you **won't** fit into their busy lives and you **won't** get a lot of quality time together. If you're a busy bee yourself, you might fall into the trap that many relationships fall into these days. I mean the trap of being so busy that quality time is almost nonexistent. This can be very detrimental to a relationship. A successful relationship thrives on the closeness that comes with time spent together. Busy Bees are sometimes lonely and looking to fill an unhappy void in their lives. So they keep their lives busy to avoid dealing with these problems. Busy Bees often have traits similar to _Career Searchers_. So, if you have a date with a Busy Bee, don't forget your day planner - you'll need it to schedule an appointment with her for your next intimate hour together.

Career Searchers

These types of girls are generally so into searching out their careers, that it is all they talk about. I'm going to school for this or I'm studying for that or I'm moving to another city or state to get a job. These girls are so wrapped up in their future, they forget about the present. And they're so caught up in climbing the ladder of success, that their careers come first, **not you!** So if you enjoy being second to her career and not knowing what and who is more important to her, date a Career Searcher and she'll certainly confuse you. Relationships with these types of girls usually don't last long. So let these girls search for their careers and themselves on their own.

Cell Phone Chicks

Well I guess this is the cell phone generation...and it's here to stay! When you go on a date with a Cell Phone Chick, you can kiss your undivided attention goodbye. This is the type of girl who considers all her cell phone calls first priority and you a definite second. It appears that so many chicks can't go one minute without talking to someone on the cell. Is this just me or does anyone else get annoyed by this? I think it's very rude to keep your cell phone on while on a date or with anyone you want to have quality time with. It's very common these days to be on a date that is interrupted by a cell phone call right in the middle of dinner, a movie, a special occasion or even sex! I've also observed many couples who are eating dinner at a nice restaurant and they were both talking on cell phones at the same time! Many people don't seem to have any respect or courtesy for each other these days. So when you're on a date or intimate engagement, give your date the undivided attention they deserve and turn that damn thing off!

CELL PHONE CHICKS

Confused Chicks

Oh God, get away! Confused chicks are all over the place, mentally and physically, changing jobs and moving to different towns, states, and anywhere that's different than the place they're in. Confused Chicks have no idea what they want, now or in the future. They think they do, and they'll tell you that they're going to do this and that, but they never follow through! They're confused and constantly looking for something new that will make them temporarily happy until they find the "next thing" to move on to. Confused Chicks are just that, confused! Often they will date guys who they can cling on to for some stability. But Confused Chicks generally don't last long in relationships because they're so screwed up in the confusion that they cause themselves. Some of their other CD traits may be found in _Messy Car Girls, Problem Chicks, Disorganized Chicks, Picky Undecided Orderer,_ and _Unreliable Chicks._ Eventually, a Confused Chick might find some stable independence, but believe me, if you date a Confused Chick, you'll be one helluva confused guy.

Controlling Chicks

Well I'm sure you've met one or two of these chicks in your life. They are very similar to controlling guys. Controlling Chicks enjoy being in charge of as many situations as they can possibly handle, For the most part, they feel they are always right. And they will stick to their guns. At times, they can be stubborn, opinionated, and of negative behavior, and have to have the last word. Controlling Chicks generally don't get along well with controlling guys. That would be like putting two bulls in a pen. So they are much more compatible with a passive guy who doesn't mind being put in his place, told what to do, and how to do it. Some of the CDs she may enjoy the company of are _Gold Diggers_, _Mystery Women_, and _Opinionators_. So, if you are the type of guy who doesn't have a backbone and enjoys being dominated and controlled, then head to your local pet store, purchase a leash and a collar for yourself, and without a doubt your loving mate will make sure it has a good **snug** fit!

Courtesy Call / E-mail Chicks

These are the girls who will call or e-mail you a few days after your first date to say hi and chat for just a few minutes, but they will keep the conversation or e-mail short. They are basically contacting you to be courteous, because they know you gave them a nice date. It's a form of guilt release and the reason they keep the conversation short is because they are not really interested in you. But they want to be courteous and acknowledge you as a nice person. Courtesy Call / E-mail Chicks won't call you a second time because that would show interest on their part. And if you ask them out for a second date during the courtesy call, chances are they will decline your invitation. So my advice to you is lay back and let her do the talking. If she is truly interested in you, she will make hints that she would like to go out again. If there are no hints, just say something like, "It was nice to hear from you, thanks for the call or (e-mail). Take care." It's always nice to have the ball in your court, so don't show too much interest.

INTERESTING NOTE: 38% of singles would pick up the phone and call the next day if they were interested in a 2nd date, after a great 1st date. 28% would wait to be pursued. SW AIRLINES SPIRIT MAG. IT'S JUST LUNCH.COM

Cursing Chicks

Now here's a girl I don't think you necessarily want to introduce to your mother. This type of girl will often curse when a problem or something of her dislike occurs. Usually, this type of girl is not necessarily the classiest of girls and most likely will be of negative behavior. But some girls use curse words repetitively and subconsciously as common practice in conversation.

Some of the phrases you might hear from a Cursing Chick are:

✶ Oh sh#t, I locked my keys in the fu#king car!
✶ That bitch is a slut!
✶ Shit! I just had 4 damn beers, and now I have to piss!
✶ (Or the classic) He's an asshole
✶ (Or maybe just a simple) Fu*k You!

CURSING CHICKS

Some of her more positive cursing statements are:

✷ Look at that baby, isn't he fu#king cute?

✷ Sh*t, you crack me up!

✷ Damn, that movie was fu#king great!

Cursing Chicks will generally socialize with <u>Negative Smokers</u>, <u>Problem Girls</u>, <u>Bull$#itter Chicks</u>, <u>Negative Gum Chewers</u>, <u>Trashy Chicks</u>, <u>Obnoxious-Loud Chicks</u>, <u>Negative Conversationalists</u> and <u>Boozer Babes</u>, and they often share some of the same characteristics. So, if you're a curser and enjoy the company of a gutter mouth, just head downtown to your local redneck dive, have a seat at the bar, order a beer, and before you know it, you'll undoubtedly meet up with a Cursing Chick whom you'll enjoy exchanging obscenities with.

Cynical Chicks

Cynical Chicks are a handful. These types of chicks are callously calculating and skeptical of the motives of others. They also have a cynical remark about almost everything you say. They are usually of negative attitude and will tear you apart if you say something negative about them. Cynical Chicks are often frustrated individuals looking for the opportunity to argue. If you try to be friendly to one, she may think to herself, "What does he want from me?" Cynical Chicks have a hard time trusting anyone and are always on the defense and ready for a snide remark.

Some examples of cynical remarks are:

✷ Good Morning Melanie, how are you? Her remark: *"Don't even ask!"*

✷ Would you like to go out some time Melanie? Then she says, *"Don't you wish!"*

✷ Melanie, you look great in those pants. Her reply: *"What are you looking at?"*

✷ Melanie, what are you doing this weekend? She answers: *"Wouldn't you like to know!"*

✷ Melanie, would you like to get married someday? Her reply: *"Hell no! I ain't marrying no man!"*

Cynical Chicks love to be in control, similar to Controlling Chicks. They often have to be right, and even if you're right, you're wrong. They must win the argument and they **will** have the last word!

Common employment positions for her are:
* Bill Collector
* Police Officer
* Jail Warden

So if you enjoy dating a Cynical Chick, just be on guard for her cynical remarks and comebacks and remember to shut your mouth, do what she says, and repeat after me . . . . . **I'm always wrong!**

Disorganized Chicks

Well this CD is pretty self-explanatory. I don't think I need to inform you that Disorganized Chicks are very frustrating to date, unless, of course, you are a disorganized guy. Then, once again, you are a disorganized match made in heaven. But I myself am an organized guy, and I feel organization would be a plus in a chick's character trait. But there are different degrees of organization, and it just depends on what degree you're comfortable with. A Disorganized Chick can drive you crazy, especially if you're in a relationship with her.

Here, I'm going to give you a few clues on how to spot a Disorganized Chick on your first date.

* If she makes you wait more than 25-30 minutes when picking her up or meeting her.
* Observe her appearance - clothing, hair, etc. Is she well put together or **not**?
* Look at her fingernails, are they chewed, chipped, broken, or just plain nasty? If so, that's a definite sign of a Disorganized Chick or perhaps just a chick who is a complete nervous wreck.
* Is her car a mess? That's a sure sign of disorganization.
* Glance into her purse if you get the chance. Is everything just thrown into it? If so, this is another strong hint of a Disorganized Chick.
* Does she frequently misplace her keys?
* Are her thoughts and actions scattered?
* Does she often lose things?

The best way to find out whether a girl is disorganized is to visit her home or apartment. This will tell you a lot about her organization level. Remember - your home reflects who you are.

Some of the CDs she may associate with are: _Messy Car Girls_, _Problem Girls_, _Schlumpy Chicks_ and _Unreliable Chicks_.

Disorganized Chicks will not only live their lives in a disorganized way, eventually they will turn **your** life upside down as well! So if you thrive on total chaos in your life, then have at it. But as for me, I have three words of advice for you - **Don't expect much!**

DISORGANIZED CHICKS

Domestic Woman

Here's a woman we haven't seen since the 1950's. All I can say is if you're looking for a domestic woman in the USA, you can just about forget it!

Remember the days when the woman used to cook dinner, take care of the home and children when the husband went to work? **Well kiss them goodbye!**

The only place you might be lucky to find a Domestic Woman is in the Asian Countries or Russia. So call your travel agent and get your passport updated because you're going overseas. Bon Voyage!

Ex-Relationship Mentioners

Oh, wow, does that bug me! This is a Dating 101 no-no. These types of women are always talking about their ex-relationships. **"Oh my ex and I came here"** or **"My ex liked to do that"** or **"You're just like my ex."** For the respect of your date, don't bring up you ex-relationships. It's immature and inconsiderate, and shows a lack of sensitivity on your part. So keep the conversation and interest on your date, and enjoy the fact that you've been asked on a date. And girls, if you're interested in a second date, keep your ex in the **past**, not on your **present** date.

Family Obsessors

Wow! These girls are a trip! A family obsessor's life revolves around her family and her family's problems. Over and over again she will find reasons why her family members need her, and her family obsessive behavior will demand a lot of her time. If you're in a relationship with a Family Obsessor, her obsession will take a toll on you, both mentally and physically.

Here I've given you some common statements a Family Obsessor might mention:

* Oh, my sister is sick, and I have to spend the weekend with her.
* I have to help my mom run some errands.
* My aunt and uncle are going through some tough times and they need my help.

* My brother and sister-in-law just got divorced, and I need to comfort them.
* My sister lost her job, and I've got to help her look for a new one.
* My mother and father are staying with me for the week.
* I'm going to the movies with my mom, dad, sister, brother and cousins . . . wanna come?

There is nothing wrong with being a loving, caring family member. In fact, it's another great character trait. But when it comes obsessive, it becomes **your problem** as well. Family Obsessors will want to draw you into their family matters, so if you're interested in dating a Family Obsessor, just be aware that you will be dating her and her entire family, as well as their problems. Have family fun!

FAMILY OBSESSORS

Feminine Ladies

Now here's a lady that's on the endangered species list. In fact, she's almost extinct. You might remember seeing this type of lady in movies from the 1940s and 1950s. Those were the last years in which she commonly walked the earth. It's so sad to see this type of classic lady gradually fade away as time moves on. Call me old-fashioned, but I, and many other guys, are really attracted to feminine females. When most guys see a girl with long hair in a dress, skirt, or any other type of feminine outfit, they are more likely to be attracted to her rather than the girl who acts, dresses and looks like a man. Even though it's very stylish and very socially accepted these days to dress fairly masculine. Femininity is not only in the way a girl dresses, but also in the way she acts, talks, and displays politeness with a bit of innocence. Southern girls are still known to have these qualities. Besides in the South, where are these rare feminine felines?

Well you might spot a few living amongst the "manly women" of our society, but some of the places they have been known to be spotted are:

* Catholic Churches
* Cooking classes
* Ballroom and Ballet dance classes
* Floral Arrangement classes

Feminine Ladies are not easily found these days, so if you have the pleasure of dating one, enjoy the experience and don't forget to be a gentleman, bring her flowers, open the car door, and surely you will flatter a Feminine Lady.

FEMININE LADIES

Gold Diggers

I'm sure you've heard of this type of woman. She is a long time classic. She is the type that is looking to be treated like a princess and wants financial security for the rest of her life and she wants to get it from you!

Some of the questions she may ask you while on the first few dates are:

✱ Your car is very nice, what kind is it?
✱ How big is your house?
✱ Is your business very lucrative?
✱ How long have you been with your company?
✱ Nice watch! What kind is it?
✱ AOL/TimeWarner is a great stock, have you any interest in stocks?

She will carefully phrase the questions. So be aware when any questions arise concerning personal finances or material possessions. She might add in her conversation that she would like to be a "stay-at-home mom." Though this is very noble, this statement could hint towards "golddiggership." Some of the CDs she may associate with are: _Hair Flippers / Mirror Lookers_, _High Maintenance Women_, and _Users_, So if you're interested in dating a Gold Digger, just get ready to whip out the credit cards, the big diamond ring and join the ranks of the many men who fell into the Gold Digger Trap.

GOLD DIGGERS

Gum Chewers

There are 2 different kinds of Gum Chewers.

Type A: The positive Gum Chewer. This type of girl will typically chew gum before a social occasion or after a meal so she can feel confident while being engaged in close contact conversation. Usually she will choose a small, fresh mint type of gum. She will chew with her mouth closed in a ladylike fashion. This is the type of girl who is prepared. I'm impressed!

Type B: The negative Gum Chewer. This type of girl usually has an attitude; She will chew quickly and sometimes aggressively, often with her mouth open. She can also be a gum popper and bubble blower and is generally annoying. These types of girls can be nervous and habitual, similar to the Nervous Smoker. Aggressive, nervous Gum Chewers really don't impress me very much. In fact, they irritate me - especially during a movie. So if you enjoy hanging out with a bubble-popping, lip-smacking, jaw-chomping chick, just head to your local convenience store and pick her up a pack of Bubble Yum so she can chew and blow 'til her jaw's content.

BLEH!

GUM CHEWERS

Hair Flippers / Mirror Lookers

If your date looks in the mirror more than 2 or 3 times a night, this says only one thing **insecure high maintenance woman.** There is nothing wrong with making sure you look good, but these types of women have an obsession with primping their hair and makeup. I'm sure it's a sign of insecurity or vanity of some sort. These types of women are constantly looking at themselves whenever they get the opportunity.

Some samples of these types of women's behavior include looking excessively into:

* Rearview mirrors
* Bathroom mirrors
* Compact mirrors
* Window reflections

So if you're dating a Hair Flipper / Mirror Looker. I'm sure her habit will become a pain in your ass eventually.

High Maintenance Women

I could write an entire book on these types of chicks. High Maintenance Women can be spotted in every corner of the world, from ghetto to royalty. High Maintenance is a state of mind and attitude. So she may not have financial wealth, she just has to have the best she can get, as often as she can get it, and in any may she can obtain it. Remember that there are different types of high maintenance women. Here are three examples of High Maintenance Women.

Type A: Self-made / High Maintenance Women: Many high maintenance women work hard to achieve success on their own, and they live their own independent high maintenance lifestyles that they have created for themselves. This can be an impressive kind of woman, but sometimes too independent, leaving you in the dust.

Type B: User / High Maintenance Women: Some high maintenance women don't have a pot to piss in, but they think everyone owes them something, so they're going to get anything they can from anyone in any way they can get it. Similar to _Users_ and _Gold Diggers_, these chicks want the best, but they're not willing to work for it. You would be classified as **insane** if you are attracted to this kind of woman!

Type C: Daddy's Girl / High Maintenance Women: These types of girls are all around us. Daddy's Girls are very high maintenance and they expect **you** to provide for them in the same way their rich daddy does.

Some of her statements she might mention are:
"My daddy bought me this BMW for graduation" or "My parents paid for my condo." Daddy is her financier in all her emergencies and needs and she's very spoiled! If you date a Daddy's Girl, **you** will be her financier as soon as your relationship becomes serious. So if you're a high dollar roller, she's the one for you. But remember one thing, you'll always be giving her the gift that keeps on giving, **your wallet!**

High Maintenance Women are pretty easy to spot, so if you go on a date with one, just be on the lookout for these obvious clues and let your own judgment tell you if this is the kind of chick you're attracted to.

if she's wearing:
* Expensive jewelry
* Designer clothing
* Designer accessories

Physical appearance:
* French manicure
* Perfect / stylish hair
* Makeup is perfect and excessive

Her conversation hints towards:
* Your finances and investments
* Her finances and investments
* What material possessions she wants to acquire
* Vacation and travel she desires
* Fine dining and wine
* Anything expensive

Her home/apartment:
* Has expensive décor
* The newest updated appliances
* Her closet has excessive amount of shoes
* Be on the lookout for her designer pet

Her High Maintenance automobile, such as:
* BMW
* Audi
* Mercedes
* Lexus
* Jaguar
* Porsche

Now that I've given you some examples of what to look for and you think you've spotted a High Maintenance Woman, the next step is to figure out which type she is and how to handle her. Here's my advice:

If she is a **"very rare", loving, caring, giving,** _Self made High Maintenance Woman_, then you've hit the jackpot. She's a keeper!

If she's very common, controlling, gold-digging, hair-flipping, mirror-looking, compulsive spending, shop-aholic, user, high maintenance chick, then may I advise you to **get the hell away from her as fast as you can!**

HIGH MAINTENANCE WOMAN

Hippie Chicks

Well, here's a chick we're seeing reappear 40 years later. This is the type of chick who is all natural, and still enjoys listening to the Grateful Dead and Bob Marley. The physical appearance of a Hippie Chick can vary. She often fashions long denim skirts, cotton dresses or hip-hugger jeans and sandals; also, she often doesn't wear any makeup or underwear. Her hair most likely will be long and sometimes she sports bushy underarms and hairy legs. Some of the things Hippie Chicks might be interested in are nature, incense, spiritual activities, marijuana, chanting, yoga, silver jewelry, vegetarian foods, and drum circles. Hippie Chicks are usually friendly, low maintenance, and liberal minded about sex and drugs. And, they are generally attracted to earthy, hippie guys. So if you want to date a Hippie Chick, grow your hair out, put on a pair of sandals, bell bottoms and an Indian import cotton shirt, and head to your nearest bead or head shop, health food or spiritual book store. Light up a joint, put on a smile and act mellow, and you might just get lucky. Some of the CDs Hippie Chicks often enjoy the company of are _Spiritual Chicks_ and _Laid-Back Attitude Chicks_. But just remember one thing, the 60s are over!

HIPPIE CHICKS

Holy Roller Chicks

These are the types of girls who are very religious. Now let me tell you that there is nothing wrong with being spiritual or religious in any way. But when it becomes fanatical, it becomes strange. Holy Roller Chicks are all about being obsessed with their church functions and church friends. It's all they talk about. Praise this and praise the Lord for that. Holy Roller Chicks are generally in search of holy roller guys who go to church consistently and attend church activities and Bible studies at least twice a week. So if you're in search of a Holy Roller Chick, take your bible in one hand and your church activity program in the other hand, head to your local church, find a Holy Roller Chick, and start saying your prayers. Amen!

HOLY ROLLER CHICKS

Ice Cream Buyer Babes

This is the type of girl who displays a good sign of reciprocation, similar to _Popcorn Buyers_ and _Automobile Door Unlockers_. These girls are often very caring and giving and have great potential for a long lasting relationship. Ice Cream Buyer Babes will gladly offer to buy both of you an ice cream cone during "THE WALK" after a movie or dinner date. A very responsible girl will do this, thus making for a very sweet date.

Interested Girls

Ok, now here's a positive one. How do you know when a girl is interested in you? I could go on and on writing about this one. But let me give you a few helpful hints. First of all, a girl will show her interest in you in quite a few ways. **Let me give you the most obvious clues:**

* If you're in a social situation, and a girl looks at you and smiles, that's the first hint that she may want you to approach her - _This is a good sign, at least someone's checking you out!_
* If you meet a girl and start to converse, and she begins to smile, laugh, and touch you gently on the hand or shoulder. _This is another good sign of interest. Enjoy It!_
* If while having a conversation, she asks you sincere questions about yourself - interests, likes, dislikes, etc. _This is a definite sign that she wants to get to know you and is interested in you. This is great, how cool!_
* If she mentions that she would like to see a certain movie or go to a specific place. _This is a major hint that she wants you to ask her out._
* If a girl mentions that your cologne smells nice or she asks what kind of cologne you are wearing. _This is a sign that she's noticing you. That's a good thing!_
* If a girl goes to the ladies room and then returns to talk To you, that's a positive sign. If she returns looking a little more primped. _That's a definite sign she wants to look attractive for you and is interested. Yeah baby!_
* If while engaging in conversation, you mention your type

of job, work or business and she asks for your business card and even asks for your help with something related to your line of work, for **example**: *"Oh, I could really use some help with my computer"* or *"Do you do tune-ups?"* This is another sign of interest.

* If she speaks positively to you about you and your interests and compliments you in any way. *This is a sure hint of interest.*

* If a girl approaches you, even if it's a subtle approach, with any type of question about yourself. **Heads up** it could be her way of trying to get your attention.

* If you offer her your business card and she looks at it with disinterest and she takes the business card and quickly stuffs it into her purse or leaves it on a table without really looking at it. *You can be sure of one thing - she is NOT interested!* **Move on!**

If a girl is flirting with you, she may show interest through her body language such as:

* Twirling her hair seductively
* Crossing her legs in an obvious way
* Turning her body around in a sexy way
* Smiling and staring at you
* Showing her cleavage obviously
* Laughing and joking with you
* Teasing you
* Touching you on your hand, back or shoulder

Sometimes girls are very subtle and sometimes they are very bold in their approach. But don't forget to look for the most important clue of all: **Is she wearing an engagement or wedding ring on the fourth left-hand finger? Or is there a tan line where that ring was?** If so, she may be out to do a little harmless flirting and may have no genuine interest in you at all. On the other hand, she may be interested in having an affair, which could lead to confusion, trouble and heartache. So I have two words of advice for you, **Be Aware!**

Intelligent Women

Here's a chick that will keep you on your toes! Intelligent Women can be a great mind-stimulating date. That is, if you are an intelligent guy. She will discuss many types of topics and is aware of all that is going on in world events. She can be a good arguer, so don't try to be right all the time because chances are you will be put in your place with intelligence.

Intelligent Women are great to date, but if your intellect is not up to par, you will probably bore her.

Some of the places you may encounter an Intelligent Woman are:

* Medical Universities
* Libraries
* Law Firms
* TV News Studios
* Political Events
* Chess Matches

So, if an Intelligent Woman is what you are after, just apply for a job at NASA and surely you'll hook up with an Astronautical Engineer Babe!

Laid-Back Attitude Chicks

Now I'm not talking about the lazy chick who falls asleep on the sofa while watching her soaps and eating Twinkies. I'm talking about a girl who has a relaxed disposition and displays a calmness in her actions and mannerisms. Relaxed people in general exude confidence and patience, and this is a very sexy and attractive personality trait, for anyone male or female, younger or older.

Laid-Back Chicks are often good listeners and tend to have a mature-minded relaxed attitude through life's ups and downs. These types of girls make great relationship partners, but are hard to find because many are already snatched up. Some of the places you might encounter a Laid-Back Attitude Chick are bookstores, the beach, yoga classes, jazz clubs, wine tastings, and church. But they can be found almost anywhere, if you are aware enough to spot one. So if you're a laid-back type guy and want to find a girl with the same type of disposition, then be on the lookout for a relaxed laid-back chick and the two of you can live a nice, healthy, relaxed life together. If you're a hyperactive guy, it's possible a relaxed chick might be the one to balance out your energy. But if your relaxed date is freaked out by your hyper-activity, I suggest you have a couple of glasses of wine, practice some deep breathing exercises and listen to a Depok Chopra meditation cd before you go on a date with a relaxed, laid-back chick.

Macho Chicks

Now here's a chick that can handle her own! Macho Chicks are of masculine mind, but there are different levels of Macho Chicks. They can range from tom-boy to body slamming wrestlers. Though some can appear feminine on the outside, they can be very macho on the inside and for some guys this is a big turn-on. Macho Chicks are basically of macho mind and spirit and can also be physically macho as well. Let's just say that their testosterone level is a bit higher than that of an average female.

HELP!

MACHO CHICKS

Some of the obvious indicators of classic stereotypical female machismo are as follows:

Clothing

if she's sporting:
* A T-shirt with the sleeves rolled up or cut off
* Jeans with a black studded belt and black boots to match
* Spurs on her boots (country girl macho)
* Thick silver chain that hangs from pocket to wallet
* Hanging keys clipped to the belt loop of her jeans
* Baseball cap worn backwards

Habits

Does she frequently:
* Spit
* Yell out loud
* Scratch herself
* Belch
* Keep a pencil behind her ear
* Keep her hands in her front pockets
* Act aggressive
* Carry a macho stance
* Throw a punch at you just for fun
* Stick her fingers in her mouth and whistle loudly

Personal Transportation

She commonly drives a:
* Pickup truck
* Motorcycle
* 4-wheel drive Jeep
* Tractor Trailer

Physical Appearance

She will most likely fashion:
* Very short masculine hairstyle
* A walk with a bob-like hop
* A masculine physique
* Little or no makeup

Employment Positions

* Police Officer
* Jail Guard
* Mechanic
* Truck Driver
* Construction Worker
* Gym Teacher
* Landscaper
* Welder
* Wrestling Instructor
* Cable TV Installer
* Personal Trainer
* Military Drill Instructor

Macho Chicks can be spotted almost anywhere, and some of the most popular Macho Chick hangouts are:

* The gym
* Sports events (example: boxing, arena football, hockey games)
* Pool halls
* Motorcycle and auto races
* WWF events
* Kickboxing classes

By now you should have a general indication of what Macho Chicks are about. There are all types of women out there and some are better suited for others, but Macho Chicks can be very helpful in a relationship.

Some of their many helpful qualities are:

* If you get a blowout while driving down the highway, she will be more than happy to fix your flat.
* If you're experience plumbing problems, a Macho Chick will be right there to fix your leaky faucet.
* If you get in the mood to go four wheeling or mud bogging, she's ready to go when you are.
* If you get in a fight with your buddy and you're losing, your Macho Babe can pack a mean punch.
* If you want a weight lifting buddy, she'll be right there to spot you.
* If you need a beer drinking football buddy, she'll be glad to crack open a beer and turn on the big screen TV.

So if you're a macho kind of guy or just a guy that enjoys an iron pumping, football throwing, basketball dunking, body slamming kind of chick, this is the chick for you . . .knock yourself out!

Mental Abuse Takers - MAT

This is an incredibly frustrating topic. I see it all the time, and MATs are plentiful in our society these days. I don't understand why girls date guys who don't respect them and treat them poorly. It seems increasingly common for girls of all ages to be in relationships with guys who don't care about their needs. MATs seem to subconsciously enjoy being controlled and treated with demeaning disrespect and are in constant need of acceptance. MATs generally subconsciously seek out the mental abuse type of guy. So if you're one of the "nice guys", don't worry about attracting a MAT, because she's not interested in being treated with respect. So she won't be attracted to you. She's on a mission for a guy who will mentally and emotionally abuse her in just the way she wants. So the question remains, why does this happen? Is it her upbringing? Is it the time in which we live? Or maybe it's that she has no self-respect. So, whose fault is it? I can't say it's entirely the guy's fault, because if a girl allows this type of abuse to take place in her life, she's just asking for trouble. If anyone male or female is accepting recurring abuse in his or her life, this is not an emotionally stable person and you don't want to date them. I've often asked girls, "So why do you stay with him if he's not treating you right?" and the most common answer is "Because I love him." **This is the most insecure, mentally and emotionally dysfunctional statement I've ever heard.** MATs have absolutely no clue of what love is. I'm not a psychologist, but I know one thing. If a person doesn't know how to receive love and respect themselves, they won't be able to reciprocate love and respect. MATs have deep rooted insecurities and it's a sad and serious mental illness. Though they might appear normal outwardly, inwardly they are of ill nature. And of course, let us not forget that guys can also be a MAT personality as well.

Now let me give you a few of the most common clues to look for when you come in contact with a potential MAT:

* If she speaks of past relationships or parents who were abusive in any way
* If she repeatedly puts herself down
* If it's obvious that she has low self-esteem

You might ask why a woman would stay with a guy who treats her so poorly?

These are some of the basic justifications I've observed through countless hours of dating conversations with MAT women I've met.

* He earns big bucks.
* He is good looking and tall.
* He has an impressive image.
* He has a great body.
* He has a power position.
* He's very cool.
* He's popular.
* He's a big talker (bull$#itter).
* Sex is great.
* I can change him. (The most popular and absurd reason of all)

If a girl constantly accepts these types of behavior from a guy, then she would be considered a MAT.

She accepts and stays with him even though:

* He displays lack of respect.
* He doesn't show interest in the things she wants to do.
* He will put her down verbally in public.
* He doesn't remember important dates
    example: birthdays, anniversaries, etc.
* He has to have it his way most of the time.
* He doesn't pay much attention to her; he ignores her.
* He shows lack of affection, except when he wants sex.
* He is insensitive to her needs.
* He doesn't keep his promises.
* He is unfaithful.
* He doesn't listen to her.

OK so now you have some examples to help you identify women with MAT personalities. If this type of personality turns you on, then you, too, may enjoy being mentally abused. Once again I say, have at it! But first I have a few words of advice for you. Well for the guys; Start appreciating and respecting your girlfriend or wife. For girls; Don't let the guys get away with any of these disrespectful acts! If you do, then you're not respecting yourself.

One last note: You need to make sure that your date wants to be treated with respect. If you accept anything less, you're setting yourself up for all kinds of problems. And remember it's not healthy to be treated like a **door MAT**!

Messy Car Girls

These girls are very common. When dating a girl, check out her car. Is it neat or messy? If it's messy, you can be sure she's not really an organized girl.

Examples:
* Food wrappers, bottles and cans on the floor
* Laundry and clothes thrown in the back seat
* School books in a disorganized mess
* Kids toys strewn about
* Dirty windows and interior
* Ash tray is full of cigarette butts
* Trunk is full of unnecessary, scattered items

Messy Car Girls are a sign of a disorganized person and it's probably a hint of a disorganized lifestyle. If you go out in her car and she throws stuff from the front seat to the back, that is a strong sign of a messy, disorganized person. Be cautious with Messy Car Girls, their whole lives can be a mess as well.

MESSY CAR GIRLS

Moms with Kids

OK, now here's a sensitive topic! Moms with kids are usually very dedicated to their children, which is a very healthy and noble character trait. But the problem is they often become obsessed with their offspring, like as if they're married to them. And they rarely make quality time to spend with their boyfriend or go on a date. The answer here is Single Mothers need to make time to date and spend quality time with their significant other!! Otherwise, you will never have time to get intimate and have a serious healthy relationship.

These are some of the statements a Mom with kids might say: "I can't go out with you tonight because":

* I have to take my son to soccer practice.
* My daughter has cheerleading rehearsal and she needs me there.
* I have to drop off my children at my ex-husband's house.
* My son isn't feeling well, I can't leave him alone.
* I'm taking the kids to the movies, doctor, concert, friend's house, etc., etc., etc.

On and on and on you will have a very tough time trying to get her alone and if you finally do get into that intimate moment with her . . . "Riiiiiing" goes the cell phone...MOM I NEED YOU FOR . . . ??? WHATEVER! And you'll have to be patient and deal with it. So all I can say to you is this, if you want to date a Mom with kids it would probably be best if you also had kids, so you can relate, join in and start your own baseball team and be one happy family, just remember....Think BRADY BUNCH

Mystery Women

Mystery Women are very similar to mystery men. They don't speak much about their past and don't give you any specifics on themselves. They keep you wondering and are full of mental/mystery games. They are generally cool, calm and quiet and they want to have some kind of mental control over you by keeping you in the dark. This is not a healthy act for a future partner. This mystery could fall into other areas of her personality and always keep you guessing and make you very frustrated. It makes me wonder what they are hiding and then I have a trust problem. Mystery women make me feel uncomfortable. The only way to keep one step ahead of a mystery woman is by being a mystery man, and then let the games begin!

Needy Cling-ons

Here's a woman that will have you running for the exit faster than you can say co-dependent. Needy Cling-ons are a very common personality type. This is the type of woman who will draw you into her life and cling on to you as fast as possible. "Do I sense desperation?" In other words, **she wants a man!** And if it's you she wants, she will do whatever it takes to get you.

Here are some examples of a Needy Cling-ons' techniques used to cling on to you:

* Dressing seductively with a short skirt and plenty of leg and a low cut blouse with plenty of cleavage for you to drool on.
* Showering you with little gifts, stuffed animals, etc.
* Sending you love notes or cards.
* Cooking you a great romantic dinner.
* Giving you great sex.

Now that her spell has you in a euphoric trance and she's attracted you into her clingy, needy web of desire, this is when she digs her co-dependent claws into your life and thus begins your transformation from man to mouse.

These are some of the questions and statements a Needy Cling-on woman may ask you after she has you wrapped around her needy cling-on finger:

* So, why didn't you call me when you got home from work? (I called you 5 times)
* Don't you think we should move in together?
* All my friends are getting married.
* Where are we going for our first week/month anniversary?
* I wish you were more romantic.
* Why don't we spend more time together?
* Isn't that engagement ring beautiful?
* Look at those cute children, you'd be such a great father.

The sickest, psycho cling-on statement of all:

* Guess who's going to be a daddy?

Needy cling-ons are like monkeys: They don't let go of one vine until they have hold of the next. So my advice to you is to read her carefully **before** jumping into her needy, clingy clutches or you'll need to cling on to a one-way ticket outta there!

JUST A LITTLE NOTE BEFORE I FINISH; 46% OF FEMALES START USING THE WORD "BOYFRIEND" AFTER 10 DATES, 6% WILL USE THE TERM AFTER 3 DATES... THOSE WOULD BE CONSIDERED THE NEEDY CLING-ONS

NEEDY CLING-ONS

Negative Conversationalists / Whiners

This type of woman will talk about all her troubles and how she doesn't like her job or situations in her life: "I wish I had this" or "Why can't I get that" or "It's too cold in here" or "I don't like the food, movie or whatever" Whine, whine, whine! She just doesn't have any enthusiasm or positive thoughts towards anything. She whines incessantly and you feel you could never make her happy. Whiners love to find things to complain about; so if you enjoy hearing your date bitch about everything, go for it! But before you do, let me give you some simple words of advice. Negative Conversationalists/Whiners are a pain in the ass, move on!

No Personality Chicks

This is the type of girl who is very quiet. When you go out on a date and try to have a conversation, she basically will answer yes or no to most of your questions. Instead of asking her a question with yes or no answers, try rephrasing it so that she can elaborate a bit. No Personality Chicks are tough to be on a date with. I've been on a few dates with a No Personality Chick, and I've taken her to rock concerts, Disney World, IMAX movies, etc. I tried and tried to get a reaction out of her, but to no avail. Talk about frustrating! It drove me nuts! I just threw my hands up, and said to myself, "Some chicks just have no personality and there's nothing you can do to change that." You can try and try to get her to have a response to something, but unfortunately, she has the personality of a comatose patient.

Obnoxious-Loud Chicks

This is the type of chick that is loud, obnoxious and IN YOUR FACE when she gets drunk or excited in any way. These types of chicks have absolutely no control over their vocal volume and have no clue that they're being rude, obnoxious and loud. Obnoxious Loud Chicks get real close to your face while conversing and can be an embarrassment to your friends and family. I wouldn't recommend bringing an OLC to any type of formal function; however, you might try taking her to a boxing match or a WWF event. I'm sure she'd fit right in! These types of chicks are often hyper, smoke, drink, curse and are a nervous wreck! So make sure you are wearing your ear plugs and goggles when conversing with an Obnoxious-Loud Chick, because her spit often flies in every direction, including your face!

The Opinionators

These types of women always seem to have a strong opinion and a direct answer on many issues.

They might say:
* "I don't think what he/she did was right!"
* "What the government is doing is wrong!"
* "I definitely don't agree with that!"
* "Why did you do that?" "You should do it this way!"
* "Shut up, you don't know what you are talking about!"

Over and over again, they will tell you what their opinion is on everything whether you ask for it or not. These types of women often have to have it their way and want to be in control. They can also be stubborn and argumentative. You must constantly be on guard when dating an opinionator. My opinion is, dump her!

Organized Girls

Organized girls are very impressive. These types of girls generally have it all together. Their homes are neat, their cars are clean, and they have good organized lifestyles. It's great to have a relationship with an organized girl because she can be a great asset to you in many ways. She will usually take control of timing issues, planning events, handling finances, etc. The only negative aspect of an organized girl is that sometimes she can be obsessively organized, and if you aren't equally as organized, you might find that you are incompatible with her. To spot an organized girl, observe the way she dresses and notice her attention to details. If her wallet and purse are also organized, that's a great indication of an organized girl. An organized girl is generally on time and takes pride in her life and has a strong potential for a serious relationship. I recommend dating an organized girl. Just think, if you marry her, you'll never have to worry about balancing your checkbook.

Pet Owner Obsessors

These are the types of girls who are obsessed with their pets, almost as if they were her children. Her whole life revolves around her cats, dogs, birds, goldfish or whatever. She might mention "My pet knows me best" or "No one understands me like FuFu." I think it's because she doesn't understand herself and she feels her pet does, and consoling with her pet calms her nerves and often fills a relationship void. Obsessive pet owners are strange and difficult to have a relationship with. If you date a Pet Owner Obsessor, you will become second to her pet, unless you too are an obsessive pet owner. Then may I suggest you both hook up and start a breeding farm.

The Picky Undecided Orderer

This is the type of girl who, when you take her out to dinner, will change her order a few times before the dinner actually comes to the table.

She will ask the server:

* "Do you have this?"
* "How is it prepared?"
* "What kind of spices and sauces do you use?"
* "I don't like this, it's too spicy?"
* "Is this boiled or fried?"
* "I don't like the smell of this!"
* "It doesn't look like the picture!"
* She may even spit it out in her napkin

And after she receives the meal, she'll ask the server, "Can I change my order?" "This isn't what I thought it would be." Picky Undecided Orderers have the ability to drive you nuts, so I suggest you try to be as patient as possible and then think this date over. Do you really want to deal with a Picky Undecided Orderer every time you go out to eat? I guess it just depends on what your patience level is. I don't know about you, but I see a possible red flag!

Popcorn Buyers

When you take your date to the movies and you both head to the snack bar, and she says "Let me buy the popcorn," then you think to yourself, 'Wow, what a nice chick' and you say "Thanks for offering, but I've got it." Popcorn Buyers are very similar to _Auto Door Unlockers_ and _Ice Cream Buyers_, these types of girls are generally courteous and giving and these days that's very rare. You can thank your lucky stars that you're on a date with a thoughtful girl. Enjoy your date with a Popcorn Buyer, she has the potential for being a great relationship partner and remember-easy on the butter!

Positive Chicks

Now here's a great chick to date! A Positive Chick is similar to a _Smiler & Laugher Chick_. She is generally happy, fun, and full of positive energy for you to enjoy. Positive Chicks enjoy almost anything and will always make you feel good! I can't say enough good things about these types of girls. They will always see the glass as half full as opposed to half empty, and they are willing to make you happy. Some of the CD personalities she'll most likely associate with are _Ice Cream Buyer Babes_, _Automobile Door Unlockers_ and _Popcorn Buyers_. Positive Chicks are rare, so if you're lucky enough to spot one, my advice is to snatch her up as quickly as you can and she'll positively be a great date!

Present Buyers

Present Buyers are very nice girls, but are similar to _Needy Cling-Ons_. These are the girls who will buy you a present or send you a card on the second date. This is okay, but not too soon! It could scare the pants off your date **(and not in a good way)** if you're not equal in you feelings. So just relax and communicate the best you can and remember to take it slow!

PRESENT BUYERS

Problem Girls

These girls are freaks! These types of girls are always having problems in their lives. Their boyfriends or husbands treat them like crap (and they subconsciously enjoy it) and they're always telling you how everyone is taking advantage of them. These types of girls are often disorganized, smoke, chew gum, have tattoos, piercings and children. Their cell phones ring constantly from friends with more problems. They don't last long in relationships, jobs or apartments. They don't reciprocate favors because they're too caught up in their own messed up, complicated, troubled lifestyles that they have created for themselves. Their lives revolve around themselves and their troubled friends. Some of the CDs they associate with are: _Negative Smokers, Attitude Chicks, Messy Car Girls, Sickly Chicks, Unreliable Chicks, Boozer Babes, Cursing Chicks, Disorganized Chicks, Trashy Chicks_ and _Mental Abuse Takers._ These types of girls are always setting themselves up for more problems and they want to suck you into their troubled webs. I have to words of advice for you - **Get out!**

Radio Channel Changers

These types of girls are generally fidgety. They must change the radio station after every song. Constantly looking for a song or radio station they like. Generally, these girls are young, but they exist in all ages. This is a sign of a very hyper, impatient, nervous person. It's ok to surf on your own, but when you're on a date, it can be distracting and annoying. Girls: Keep the channel surfing to a minimum - find a station and keep it there! Especially if you're on a date in his car. Maybe it's just my pet peeve.

Romantic Women

Romantic Women are wonderful women to date... that is if you enjoy romance. A romantic woman will cook you a special dinner, light the candles and play soft sexy music. Oh yeah! That's my kind of woman! In return, you might want to light some candles in the bathroom and fill the bath tub with bubbles and rose petals. Don't forget the whipped cream and

strawberries and surely you will have a night to remember!
Let me give you a few more tips to light up your romantic babe.

* Roses are a MUST
* Picnic in a quiet park
* Sexy tasteful lingerie
* A quiet dinner at a nice restaurant
* A bottle of wine and cook her dinner
* Massage her feet in candlelight
* Surprise her with a gift

Romantic Women are loving and caring, so enjoy her and treat her with love, respect and as much romance as she desires and she will love you all the way home.

Schlumpy Chicks

Here's a chick who's very easy to spot. Schlumpy Chicks are the kind of chicks who are often sluggish, sloppy, lazy and generally overweight. They usually dress in baggy clothing

SCHLUMPY CHICKS

and are notorious for dragging their feet. Schlumpy Chicks can be either very nice or very negative girls and can sometimes be very intelligent. But on a 1 to 10 scale, generally their energy level is a whopping 1.

Some stereotypical employment positions they hold are:
* Delivery person
* Fast food cashier
* Kitchen help
* Convenience store clerk
* Auto parts stock person
* Truck driver

So if you're attracted to a Schlumpy Chick, just keep an open eye for this slow moving target, put on a pair of loose pants that fall down to the crack of your ass, and don't forget your flip flops so you can drag your feet right into her schlumpy life.

Serious Susans

Serious Susan is my name for a girl who is very serious. She is the type who talks about business, banking, work, news, and all things serious - similar to an _Uptight Chick_. It's very hard for you to make her laugh, and when she does laugh, it seems labored. Serious Susans often enjoy watching CNN, tracking mortgage rates, and discussing world events. They can be so serious at times, that it takes all the fun out of your date. You may get so frustrated that you just want to say "Lighten up, will ya?" I never enjoy a date with a Serious Susan. It's a chore to make her laugh, and do you want this chore all your life? I don't think so! Observe these types of women before asking them on a date. Life is too short to be with a Serious Susan, unless you're an Accounts Payable Administrator.

Sickly Chicks

These are the types of girls who are always whining that they can't go out because they're sick with something. Time and time again, they will come up with new sicknesses or physical problems to whine about. These types of girls are usually lazy, negative and just want attention.

Some of the sickly statements these hypochondriacs might mention are:

✳ "I don't feel good. I think I'm coming down with something"
✳ "I'm so tired. I'll call you back after I take a nap"
✳ "I can't go out because I have a headache"
✳ "I'm not in the mood to do [whatever]. I think I have food poisoning"
✳ "I think I'm getting my period. I feel bloated"

After she's done informing you of all the illnesses she has, the only place you will want to take your sickly date is to the doctor.

Slutty Chicks aka - Slut

A Slutty Chick is stereotypically the type of chick who enjoys sex frequently and with many partners. She commonly smokes, drinks excessively, curses and dresses distastefully. Although there are many different types of sluts, I think most guys should experience and date a Slutty Chick at least once in their life. Slutty Chicks can be so much fun - for a short while that is. You can experience life on the wild and crazy side and get it out of your system and say you did it (or her) - if you want. Slutty Chicks exist in all ages and cultures, but the good ole USA has the cream of the crop!

Slutty Chicks can be found in many places, some of the most common places are:
* Topless dance clubs
* Biker bars
* Tattoo parlors
* Redneck bars
* Adult novelty shops in the toy section

There are also many different slut types:
* Country Sluts
* City Sluts
* Young Sluts
* Old Sluts
* Biker Sluts
* White Trash Sluts
* Sophisticated Sluts
* Bar Sluts
* Alcoholic Sluts
* Office Sluts
* Banker Sluts
* Newly divorced Sluts
* Porno Sluts
* Professional Sluts (aka prostitutes)

By now you should have a good indication of where to find a Slutty Chick and also the different types of slutty chicks. But let me give you a little more information about this

"Lady of the Evening." Slutty Chicks can dress in the classic chaps, ripped jeans, tied up t-shirt with no bra, or a mini-skirt, tank top and high heels. But don't let this fool you, As some of the most conservatively dressed banker, lawyer chicks could suck the chrome off a trailer hitch (so to speak).

So if a Slutty Chick is what you are dreaming of, then head to your local titty bar, bring a bunch of dollar bills and you'll have a wide variety to choose from. You might even get lucky and meet up with a _Boozer, Smoker, Attitude, Bull$#itting, Cursing, Gold Digging, Hair Flipper / Mirror Looking, Messy Car, Disorganized, Gum Chewing, Using, Problem Girl, Trashy Slut!_ **And she would be a catch!**

SLUTTY CHICKS

Smilers & Laughers

Now here's a refreshing date to be on. Smilers & Laughers are the types of girls you want to be around. These girls will often laugh and smile when you are conversing. This makes for a very fun, happy and positive date. Smilers & Laughers enjoy life in general and are often easy to please; this can make you feel very confident. This type of personality, male or female, can have a very positive outlook in all situations, making for a healthy and happy relationship. Smilers & Laughers make you feel wanted and comfortable. These are the types of people you want to befriend. Some of the other character traits they may possess are found in _Popcorn Buyers, Ice Cream Buyer Babes, Automobile Door Unlockers,_ and _Positive Chicks_. I highly recommend dating a Smiler & Laugher, because you'll be smiling and laughing all night long.

SMILERS & LAUGHERS

Smokers

There are two types of smokers.

Type A
The relaxed smoker:

This is the type of woman who will occasionally light up a cigarette after a social engagement. She will only smoke on occasion and when she does, she will usually smoke a thin Virginia Slims type of cigarette. She's mainly smoking for the relaxing and classic effect of it. This is a cool, relaxed, calm and classic smoker.

For a smoker type of girl, this is as good as it gets.

Type B
The nervous smoker.

This is the type of woman who will light up after dinner or a movie, in her car, or any chance she gets. Lunch breaks are very important to her - and it's not because she is hungry! Smokers tend to congregate, so if you date a nervous smoker and you want to spend quality time together, you may want to consider becoming a nervous smoker yourself. If you date a nervous smoker, just be prepared for her bad breath, smelly clothing, and yellow nicotine-stained teeth. Oh yeah, and don't worry about the phlegm cough. Once she swallows, she won't do it again for a while. So just head to your local 7-eleven and buy her a lighter and a pack of Marlboro Lights and you'll surely get on her good side.

This is a touchy subject, because a lot of smokers feel there is nothing wrong with them. And a lot of pseudo normal people smoke. But I feel smokers are generally smoking because they need a short-term happiness habit. It not only effects their breath, but it's also unhealthy and denotes personal problems and a bad habit. You must make your own personal decision on whether you want to date a smoker or not. I find that smokers are generally nervous, habitual, and will have sex sooner than a non-smoker. So make the choice, to be healthy or not to be healthy, that's the question.

Spiritual Chicks

Now here's an enlightened girl who's very nice to date. Unlike Holy Roller Chicks, Spiritual Chicks aren't as fanatical about religious affairs and church functions. Spiritual Chicks are quite a bit more laid back and tend to have a more open-minded attitude towards spirituality in general. Spiritual Chicks generally become interested in spirituality in their mid-thirties and up and can be wonderful girls to date; but sometimes they can also be lost souls looking for a grasp on life. Many divorcees become Spiritual Chicks right after their divorce - looking for some solace in their lives. While Spiritual Chicks can appear as if they're living in their own world of peace and harmony and state of relaxation, they are also in touch with their inner selves and are in search of self love. This is the type of woman you want to get to know. This type of woman is often a vegetarian, is nurturing to herself, and enjoys reciprocating to her partner. Some of the places you might meet up with a Spiritual Chick are spiritual book stores, yoga classes, health food stores, spiritual conventions, and spiritual retreats. One problem which may occur when dating a Spiritual Chick is that if she's a vegetarian, her diet may consist of soy beans, barley sprouts, and wheat grass juice, which can cause flatulence, resulting in embarrassment when dining out or attending other public activities. One of the CDs a Spiritual Chick will associate with is _Hippie Chicks_. So if you enjoy the companionship of a girl who lives life in the spiritual lane, just relax on a yoga mat, light some candles and incense, put on a new age CD, do some deep breathing exercises, visualize yourself with a Spiritual Chick and lo and behold, she will appear.

Sports Chicks

Now here's an easy girl to hook up with, if you're a jock that is. Sports Chicks are all about sports, beer, and hanging out with guys and their friends at local sports bars and events. Sports Chicks can vary in shapes and sizes, from rich to poor, and from young to old. So this leaves you with a wide variety to choose from. But what do they mainly have in common? Sports Chicks are often masculine minded and love a challenge. They also enjoy crowds, friends, and being among loud enthusiastic sports fans. Sports Chicks are generally attracted to guys who are "Sport Machos." They are in their sports prime in college, but their enthusiasm about sports usually slows down in their late 20s to early 30s, after they become married to a jock and have little jock babies with baseball caps. So if you're interested in sports, and want a girl who has something in common with you, just put on a football jersey, a backwards baseball cap, and a pair of Nikes; then put on your enthusiastic macho sports attitude, grab a beer, yell real loud, high five your buddies, and surely you'll <u>score</u> a Sports Chick.

SPORTS CHICKS

Talkers - Obsessive

Here is a very common type of woman. This is the type of woman who will talk and run on and on with all kinds of stories about everything from soup to nuts. She never asks you anything about yourself nor does she show any real interest in you. When you finally get a word in, she will agree with you and then find a way to segue into her never-ending one-way conversation. If she is truly conversing **with you** and not talking **at you**, then this is a positive attribute. But if she's rambling on and on and never listens to you, or talks about subjects which have no interest to you . . . May I make a suggestion? Talk yourself into never going out with her again!

Teasers / Flirters

Well here's a girl you don't know what to do with or how to act when you're in her presence. A Teaser / Flirter will confuse the hell out of you! Every time I meet up with one, I don't know how to react. Is she interested in me? Or is she just flirting? So then I hang around, trying to figure her out and trying to make her laugh, impress her, or get more of her attention. I try to be cool, but she keeps teasing and flirting and she never gives me anything serious to grasp onto, like good conversation, a future date, her phone number or anything substantial we could do together. Teasers / Flirters often dress sexy with short skirts and low-cut blouses with plenty of cleavage. They just like to tease, flirt, look around, laugh and be cute. They aren't looking for anything serious and they mostly just enjoy the attention they desperately seek. You can't take them seriously, you just have to try to have fun with them and play their game until you're sick and tired of it and then move on. They will generally choose who they want to hang around with by the one who will give them the most attention. Nine out of ten times, they're not worth pursuing because most of the time they are too immature to pursue and they're just playing the field. So if you enjoy being frustrated and confused, a Teaser / Flirter is just the girl for you.

Touchers

Touchers confuse me. This is the type of girl who will gently touch you on your back, shoulder or hand while you are having a conversation. This makes for a very positive feeling for a guy. It makes him feel confident, and in tune with this girl. But the confusing part is whether or not this girl is touching you because she likes you or she's just a touchy person. Be observant, if she's touching almost everyone she comes in contact with, then most likely she's a **GT** - General Toucher. If she's touching only you, that's a sure sign that she's a **PT** - Personal Toucher. And that's the green light to go ahead and pursue her. Touchers are usually very warm and caring people, but can be flirtatious. So be friendly and patient when you show her interest, and she will not only touch your hand, but she may touch your heart. Aaaaaaah, how sweet!

Trashy Chicks

I'm sure we all know what type of chick this is. Trashy Chicks are a combination of character types in my bitter book, such as:

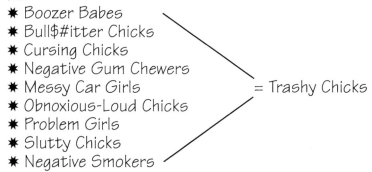

* Boozer Babes
* Bull$#itter Chicks
* Cursing Chicks
* Negative Gum Chewers
* Messy Car Girls   = Trashy Chicks
* Obnoxious-Loud Chicks
* Problem Girls
* Slutty Chicks
* Negative Smokers

So if this type of chick turns you on, just head to Jerry Springer's TV studio and I'm sure you'll have plenty to choose from.

Unreliable Chicks

Unreliable Chicks are very common in this day and age. It appears to me that many chicks are unreliable and inconsiderate to their friends, employers, and relationship partners. Although it's common practice among the younger generation, it's also prevalent in adults as well. Unreliable Chicks can be very frustrating to date.

Here are a few of the early warning signs to look for before you get too involved with this scatter brained chick.

✳ She doesn't return your phone calls or messages.
✳ She doesn't show up for your planned date.
✳ She doesn't call to let you know she's going to be late.
✳ She doesn't keep her promises.
✳ She misses important events and makes up stupid excuses why she didn't show up.
✳ She acts as though she's done nothing wrong
✳ She doesn't apologize for her forgetfulness or tardiness.

Unreliable Chicks can drive you nuts and can really mess up your plans. They often have some of the same characteristics as <u>Confused Chicks</u> and <u>Disorganized Chicks</u>. So, if you're an unreliable type of guy, an Unreliable Chick is the type who can double your unreliability. But if you're a reliable type of guy, then I suggest you buy her a day planner and teach her how to use it, have plenty of patience and don't expect her to change, Good luck!

Uptight Chicks

Uptight Chicks are just that - uptight! This is the type of chick who will make **you** feel uptight as well. While having a conversation with her, be observant of her actions.
Examples are:

✳ When you smile at her, she gives you a strained smile in return.
✳ When you make a joke, it doesn't affect her.
✳ When having a conversation with her, she'll respond with a dry a-tonal type of attitude.
✳ Her face is generally expressionless.
✳ Her lips are tight and maintain a downward frown position.
✳ Her uptight facial expressions usually cause wrinkles on her forehead.
✳ She often chews her nails.

Uptight Chicks can be of unhappy negative persona and they have a hard time relaxing and enjoying the moment.

They generally need a few stiff drinks to loosen up their spirits and then they can become a wild one. In fact, you might even find them dancing on the table with a lampshade on their head. But as soon as they sober up, it's back to being an Uptight Chick. Uptight Chicks' employment positions can vary. Some of the classic stereotypical Uptight Chicks are bankers, stockbrokers, attorneys, librarians, and accountants. But don't let this fool you, they exist in all types of backgrounds. Some of the CDs they generally associate with are _Controlling Chicks_ and _Serious Susans_. So if you enjoy the tense feeling of an ulcer, you'll certainly enjoy dating an Uptight Chick.

Users

These are the girls you probably don't want to date a second time. These girls look attractive and dressed up when you take them out and then you pay for dinner, movie, concert, or whatever. You drive and they offer nothing - not a hug or kiss. They didn't unlock your door, and they didn't even thank you for dinner or whatever: All night long, they gave you a cold attitude, and they didn't reciprocate in any way. Do you sense selfishness? Some of the CDs that they may associate with are _Gold Diggers_, _Bull$#itter Chicks_, _User High Maintenance Women_ and _Attitude Chicks_. Beware of Users. They'll be **using you** all the way to the bank.

Virgins

Now here's a girl who's definitely on the endangered species list. Virgins are becoming more and more rare as our decades progress. If you date a Virgin, the first thing you must have is PATIENCE. She'll most likely be worth the wait, but if you're a true horny dog and just can't wait to get in the sack, I don't suggest dating a virgin. It'll only lead to frustration, and HARD ACHE! So if you're on the search for a Virgin, let me give you some clues where you might find this female of purity. Some of the most common places she may be found are Bible Class, Christian College or Elementary school grades 1-6. But since you're reading this book, you're probably past that age. Perhaps you might take a trip to your local nunnery - who knows, maybe you'll get lucky!

Where to Meet Women

I have been to many different types of events and each one seems to predominantly attract a particular type of woman. So what I suggest is that you find your personality type and look for the events that will match your preferences.

These are some of the places in which I've tried to meet women:

Art Shows or gallery openings/showings: This type of event generally attracts a more mature, sophisticated type of woman. The women who attend art shows or gallery openings are typically intelligent, appreciate the fine things in life, and are stimulated by good conversation. Generally, the age range of women at this type of event is 30 and above. Some of the CD types who frequent these events are _Gold Diggers_, _Hair Touchers/Mirror Lookers_, _Laid Back Attitude Chicks_, _High Maintenance Women_, _Organized Girls_, and _Smilers & Laughers_.

Wine Tastings: Women who attend wine tastings will be very similar to the types who attend art show and gallery openings. The women who would attend a serious wine tasting tend to be even more mature. Some of the CD types who will often attend wine tastings are _Gold Diggers_, _High Maintenance Women_, _Organized Girls_, _Smilers & Laughers_, and _Touchers_.

Cruises: There are different types of cruises that attract different types of people. The types that I've experienced were more the party cruise ships like Carnival. Cruise ships may be over-rated as a way of meeting women. People have the idea that cruise ships are a romantic setting for meeting that special someone; but there is so much going on and everyone is being shuffled about, that it's very difficult to really get to know someone. If you want to meet a woman, generally you'll find her in the disco where most single people end up during the evening. It's difficult to pinpoint the type of woman you might find on a cruise, because this type of event attracts a wide variety of people from all areas of the world and in different age ranges. If you want to try a cruise, I suggest you bring along a friend. That way you'll still enjoy the cruise even if you don't meet any women who interest you.

Church: This is a place where many people will advise you is "a great place to meet women." The truth is, it may not be such a great place. The types of women who you will typically find at church vary, and a lot of people who go to church are lost souls - looking for salvation - and tend to have as many problems as people you meet in bars. A lot of women you'll likely meet in church are recently divorced and looking for a husband and possibly a father for their children. On the other hand, you will also find some quality women with good morals, family values, and a positive outlook on life. You should be aware of the personality type of women you meet in church. Because if you're not a regular church-goer and she is, this may not be a good match for you. The age range of the women you meet at church will vary greatly. The CDs you find at church may depend on the kind of church you attend. In the stricter religions, you'll find a lot of _Holy Roller Chicks_, but in the less strict religions you might find almost any type of personality.

Group Dance Classes: I highly recommend dance classes as a way of meeting women of all ages - from teens to senior citizens. It's a very fun and positive atmosphere, which makes for a non-threatening setting for getting to know someone. Women who like to dance are typically fun, happy, romantic, health conscious, and energetic. Learning to dance together somehow forms a mental and physical connection, because it requires close contact and a mutual trust. The confidence of knowing how to dance is such a positive attribute that even if you don't meet someone at dance class, your dancing skills can attract women in other social situations. Ballroom/Salsa and Swing dance classes often attract a classier type of woman than the common disco. The CDs you will probably find at these events are the _Automobile Door Unlockers_, _Positive Gum Chewers_, _Ice Cream Buyers_, _Popcorn Buyers_, _Feminine Ladies_, _Smilers & Laughers_, _Romantic Women_ and _Touchers_.

Personal Ads / Internet: I've tried both, but only to discover that it works if you like to bull$#it. So many of these ads are phony decoy ads placed to capture your attention and your money. Other ads are very sincere and honest. The trick is to figure out which is which. My rule of thumb is if she looks too good to be true in a personal ad, chances are she's probably a decoy ad put in by the ad company to entice you to call and pay their per-minute charges.

Example:

Female Swedish lingerie model 5'5", 105 lbs., long blonde hair, 36-24-36, 25 years old, no children, 6-figure income, in search of male who is fun, sexy, spontaneous between the ages of 25-60, bald men OK, pot bellies acceptable, looks not important, waiting for your $4 a minute response. (Yeah, this is a real chick - NOT!)

Then you have a REAL ad example:

Female looking for serious relationship, 45 years old, 200 lbs., 5 ft. tall, 5 children, works at Denny's, enjoys going for short drives in my '85 Ford Escort and quiet romantic nights eating ice cream, pizza, chocolate chip cookies, potato chips and watching TV. Live with retired parents in their trailer. In search of any male. Eagerly waiting to hear from you!

So if the personals are the way you choose to look for your soul mate, have plenty of patience and just be prepared to spend countless hours sifting through an endless crap shoot!

Introductions by friends and family: I'm sure many of you have experienced being introduced to a girl by a friend or family member. Generally speaking, friends of family will give it one shot to introduce you to someone they feel is right for you. If it doesn't work out, then they don't usually try a second time. There is a positive and negative side to this way of meeting the woman of your dreams.

The positive side is that your friends and family are supposed to know your personality likes and dislikes in a woman; therefore, introducing you to someone who you would be very attracted to both mentally and physically should be easy. This would seem like a very logical way of meeting a good dating match. Plus, your friends or family would most likely know this girl and should know if she is a good match for you. So all around, this seems like a positive way of being introduced to Ms. Right.

The negative side is that most of the time your friends and family don't have a clue who is a good match for you. You might have said to yourself "What the hell were they thinking when the fixed me up with this chick?" "Do they even have a clue what type of girl that I'm attracted to?" All I can say is, it's nice for them to try to hook you up, but if they can't find someone who really fits the bill, then don't even bother. The answer here is to give your match makers a complete list of your likes and dislikes and be very specific, Good Luck!

Sushi Bars: Sushi Bars are a very good place to sit and enjoy a good lunch or dinner and also converse with people who are sitting next to you (hopefully a girl you might find attractive). You will often see people eating sushi alone at a sushi bar, that's when you can start up a friendly conversation about sushi. Example: "Excuse me, but your sushi platter looks interesting, what kind is that?" or "Have you tried the salmon roll, etc., etc." thus, beginning a conversation leading to wherever you want it to go. Sushi bars are a non-threatening place where you can make friends, and people are more likely to be open to casual conversing. I also recommend getting to know the waitress/server at your favorite sushi bar or restaurant. The more women you know, the better your chances are of meeting someone you want to hook up with. So I suggest you go to the sushi bar or restaurant of your choice on a consistent basis, because it's a great way of meeting people in general.

Gym: Many of my friends are always telling me that the gym is a great place to meet single girls. As I leave no stone unturned, I joined up at my local YMCA. I consistently worked out about 3 times a week for 6 months. I talked and flirted with many women; but what I noticed was that almost all the girls I talked to were so into their workouts that they didn't want to converse at all. They were also sweaty and not looking their freshest, so I couldn't help but feel that they felt self-conscious about meeting <u>anyone</u>. A lot of people at the gym are coming and going to or from work and they really don't want to hang out and mingle. However, sometimes in the exercise classes there are breaks, and that's a good time to get a drink of water and possibly chat with the person of your desire. But as far as a place to meet someone? I say the gym is a mediocre place for possible romance to bud. It is however a great place to get in shape.

Bars: This is a classic, popular way of meeting someone special, (so to speak.) I myself have never had much luck in bars. The noise, alcohol and crowds make it very diffucult to talk and get to know someone. I suppose if you're a single boozer this is your "social heaven." The best advice I can give you is to go on Ladies Night and wait 'til they're all drunk and you might get lucky!

Bookstores: I can't count the times I've roamed around Barnes and Noble and Borders in the café section and throughout the store. I've looked and smiled at hundreds of girls over the course of time. Have I met anyone special, other than a casual conversation? <u>I don't think so</u>! I have put my time in the bookstore circuit and it hasn't worked for me. As for you, I say give it a try. It seems like a good place to meet a nice girl. Try dropping a book and maybe the girl of your dreams will offer to pick it up for you, like in the movies . . . Yeah right!

Restaurants: (get to know the waitresses and staff and go to one place consistently.)

Supermarkets: Here's another joke! Everyone says to go the supermarket and start talking to a girl over the fruit section. Ha! What a stupid thing to do. Although I've tried it many times, all I got was a strange look, and she moved on. Yeah, this gave me lots of confidence. Sorry I can't give you any good advice on this one, except try to make conversation at the checkout and if she doesn't respond, try bumping your basket into her car!

Libraries: This is a more unpretentious place to meet the woman of your desire. The library is generally quiet and relaxed, creating an intelligent, non-threatening atmosphere for all ages to meet. If you go to the library in search of love, I suggest you carry with you some kind of reading or writing material so it doesn't look obvious when you're scoping out your prey. Sit at a table, read, and check out your prospects from a distance. If you notice someone of your desire, try to make some kind of connection, either verbally or by smiling and walking in her direction. Go to the sections that interest you and you might just meet someone who has the same interests you do. In most situations someone has to make the first move, and the library is a very friendly and unexpected place to make friends. Give it a try.

Just remember, you can meet women almost anywhere and in any situation, but the trick is to be yourself and make yourself attractive to them. On page 85, I give you some examples of women's turn-ons. And if you get involved in activities in which you enjoy, the chances are good that you will attract someone who enjoys your same interests.

Here are a few more places which are popular for meeting the opposite sex . . . And <u>don't forget</u> to get there <u>early</u>, so you can relax and scope out the scenery.

* School Events
* Cafeterias
* Political Meetings
* Cooking Classes
* Bible Studies
* Seminars
* Art Festivals
* Your place of employment
* Bars / Happy Hour
* Coffee Shops (Barnies / Starbucks)
* Outdoor Concerts
* Dating Services
* Weddings
* Yoga Classes
* Poetry Readings
* Private Parties
* Dance Clubs
* Internet cafes

Top 20 Avoidance Tactics

Excuses why they don't call or can't go out . . .

20 I have friends or family visiting from out of town. *(Sounds honest)*

19 I have to work early tomorrow. *(Could be)*

18 I changed my wallet and lost your phone number. *(I guess this could be true)*

17 I'm moving this weekend. *(Common college girl excuse)*

16 I didn't get your message because my roommate didn't tell me. *(Very common excuse)*

15 I didn't get your message because my roommate/brother/friend/family member *(dog)* erased it. *(Sloppy, typical excuse)*

14 I'm going out of town. *(Doubt it)*

13 I can't do lunch because I only get a half hour and I eat at work. *(Professional excuse)*

12 I can't go out on Friday because it's girls night out. *(It's all about her)*

11 I put your number on my cell phone, and I lost my phone. *(New generation avoidance tactic)*

10 I work 7 days a week. *(She's definitely not interested)*

9 I left my wallet in my friends car and your number was in it. *(Sounds unlikely)*

8 I can't go out because my cat died. *(Aah, that's too bad)*

7 I'm waiting at the airport all day for my friends to come in. *(You could've thought of something better than that)*

6 My grandmother is in a coma. *(Pathetic excuse)*

5 I don't have a phone. *(Classic excuse)*

4 I can't go out because I'm getting and MRI. *(Rare excuse)*

3 Give me your number and I will call you. *(Yeah right)*

2 My girlfriend's boyfriend got hit by a Mack truck while riding his motorcycle and I have to comfort her. *(Aah, now she's thinking . . . this is original)*

And the number 1 avoidance tactic is:

"I have a boyfriend"
     (If I only had a buck for every time I've heard this one)

Physical Characteristics

Fingernails

Fingernails can tell you a lot about a girl's basic character. Here I've given you a few examples of what to look for when observing a girl's fingernails.

Bright and loud colors: This is generally a sign of a young and immature girl.

French Manicure: This is the sign of a classy or high maintenance girl.

Black nail polish: This is the sign of a gothic or heavy rock chick, generally young.

Bright red nail polish: This is the sign of a woman who is looking to be noticed and wants attention.

Extra long, fake nails: This is a definite sign of a distasteful, _High Maintenance Women_. Rule of thumb: The longer the nails, the higher the maintenance.

Bitten/Chewed fingernails: This is a strong sign of a troubled and nervous chick, generally _Negative Smokers_, _Messy Car Girls_, _Problem Girls_ and _Trashy Chicks_ fall into this category.

Chipped/Dirty fingernails: This is an absolute sign of a woman who works aggressively with her hands. (examples: mechanic, truck driver, construction worker or ditch digger), or else it's the sign of a plain old nasty chick.

Chipped or worn polish: Basically, this is a sign of a girl who is lazy, she also falls into the categories of _Chipped/Dirty Fingernails_, _Bitten/Chewed fingernails_, _Negative Smokers_ & _Schlumpy Chicks_.

Light Colors / Pastels: Generally the sign of a mature girl who is modest and non-pretentious. _Organized Girls_, _Feminine Ladies_, _Intelligent Women_, _Positive Gum Chewers_ fall into this category.

Dragon Nails: These are types of fingernails which are of bright coloring, fake, long, have stencils, rhinestones, and small jewelry attached to the nail. Need I say more? This falls into a category similar to _Extra long, fake nails_. But, the key words here are "distasteful and tacky!"

Natural nails, Type A: These are the type of nails that have either no polish or just a light coat of clear acrylic. She keeps them filed and clean, they are not long, but just 1/8 inch over the fingertip. This is the sign of a natural, non-pretentious tasteful kind of girl.

Natural nails, Type B: This type of girl has natural nails, but doesn't take any pride in them. Similar to _Chipped/Dirty Fingernails_, her nails are not filed and are obviously not taken care of.

Examples:
* Clipped Crooked
* One is long, one is short
* Chipped nail polish
* Cuticles are rough

These are signs of a girl who doesn't take much pride in herself and her appearance is not high on her priority list.

Skin
Observe her skin . . . Is it smooth, clean, silky, and healthy looking? If so, this is a very good sign of a woman who has good hygiene and cares about her appearance. But, if her skin is rough, dry, wrinkly with black and white heads and dried up bloody pimples, then I suggest you do not attempt to touch her - she could be hazardous to your health!

Toenails
Make sure you check out her toenails. Just because her fingernails are clean, doesn't mean her toenails are of your desire. If they are clean and polished, great! Enjoy these little piggies. But if they are chipped, cracked, smelly and her toes are nasty with toe jam, then I suggest you avoid an intimate toe kissing session.

When a girl paints her toenails the same color as her finger-nails, this is the sign of a stylish and color-coordinated girl who takes pride in her appearance, this is a positive trait in her personality. Some of her other CDs could very well be _Organized Girl_ or _Positive Gum Chewer_. But when a girl has French mani-cured fingers and toenails to match, watch out! This is the epitome of a _High Maintenance Woman_. So get ready to do some high dollar spending and serious ass kissing!

Teeth

This is very important. If her teeth are clean and white, or if she has braces, this is a sign of great hygiene and a woman who takes care of herself. But if her teeth are yellowed, black, rotted, missing or her gums are puffy and red, I suggest you get her a dental plan and avoid any French kissing.

Hair

Observe her hair . . . Is it clean, shiny, smelling fresh, and healthy looking? Or is it fried, dull, dirty, greasy, knotted and has split ends? If so, may I suggest you buy her a gift certifi-cate to a local salon (hint, hint).

Tattoos

I don't have much to say about this, except that this is a personal decision. Generally, girls who range from 18-25 are the most common candidates for this popular mainstream fad. All I can say is a vast majority of these girls are tattoo-ing themselves to be accepted and cool (like smoking), and in about ten years, most of them will be sorry they did it, and tattoo removal will be in demand. So if you're looking forward to a big blotchy ink scar on your girlfriend's or wife's body by the time she's 40, then head down to your local tattoo par-lor and surely you'll meet the tattooed chick of your dreams.

Turn-offs for Guys

Turnoffs are a personal judgment call; but here I'm giving the women some of the most popular turn-offs guys agree with.

✱ **Too much makeup:** Guy's don't like it! The key here is make-up with moderation. You don't want to look like Tammy Faye.

✱ **Too much perfume:** Once again, don't over do it. Subtleness is much more attractive. You don't want to smell like the old lady that sits next to you at church.

✱ **Excessive talking:** Guys don't like it if you ramble on and on. Some women never stop talking and they never give the guy a chance to comment. Be a good conversationalist as well as a good listener.

✱ **Clingy, smotherer:** Most guys are attracted to a semi-independent woman. Guys get turned off by a woman who appears to be needy and clingy. It mentally smothers them and will send them heading for the nearest exit.

✱ **Whining:** This is a definite turnoff for guys, or anyone for that matter. Whiners are annoying to be around, and it's a negative personality trait. Keep your whining and complaining to a minimum or he'll be walking out the door faster than he can say <u>See Ya</u>!

✱ **Flirting with other guys:** This is an absolute no-no! When you're on a date, make sure you give him the respectable attention he deserves. If you look, talk and flirt with other guys or his friends, he won't respect you. Keep your eyes and focus on him.

✱ **Bad Breath:** This is simple enough. People in general are turned off by bad breath. Make sure you pop in a fresh breath mint before and during your date, especially if you smoke and drink and then you'll be confident for that good night kiss.

✳ **Excessive drinking:** Most normal guys will be very turned off by this. If you get silly, sick or sloppy, then you'd better lay off the booze if you want to make a good impression. Getting mildly intoxicated can be fun; but if you get out of control, you could be a major turnoff to him, and putting yourself in a vulnerable position.

✳ **Aggressive and bossy:** Perhaps some guys like a bossy, aggressive chick, but as for the majority of the guys out there, this is <u>not</u> a turn-on. In fact, it's one of the most popular <u>turn-offs</u> that guys agree on. So tone down your aggressive, bossy, controlling attitude if you want another date.

✳ **Bad hygiene:** I myself have never gone on a date with a girl who had bad hygiene, but most of the guys I've spoken with have said that this is a big turnoff. Ladies, I don't think I need to be your mother and tell you to shower, and brush your teeth and hair before going on a date.

✳ **WonderBra:** This is an unexpected turnoff. I just wanted to let you girls know that making mountains out of mole hills is not the best way to impress a guy when you're in that intimate moment. He's been envisioning these larger than reality breasts, and then when he finally gets to encounter your dynamic duo, it's a major letdown and turnoff. Be careful girls!

✳ **Weight:** Most guys are not attracted to overweight or underweight women. A healthy proportional size and weight is most attractive.

✳ **Nose pickers, flatulators, belchers:** I really don't think I need to inform you on this. <u>Refer to common sense!</u>

Turn-ons for Guys

Once again, this is a personal judgment call, but most guys agree on these attributes.

✳ **Semi-independence:** Guys like it when girls are not overly independent; it makes us feel needed and wanted when we can do something for you and help you. If you are too independent, we don't feel the need to be there for you. Maybe you can just pretend to be helpless once in a while, so we can be your "Knight in Shining Armor."

✳ **Humor:** We all love to laugh and have a good time at as many opportunities as possible. Humor relaxes everyone. So make him laugh and smile as much as possible. If all else fails, take him to a comedy club.

✳ **Flirtatious:** Guys enjoy a girl who flirts honestly with us. It makes it so much easier to approach you. But don't get teasing and flirting mixed up. Teasing will only lead to frustration for a guy. Flirting may lead to friendly attraction.

✳ **Be yourself:** Let us enjoy your attractive personality - hopefully you have one!

✳ **Relaxed attitude:** A relaxed and easy going personality is a very attractive attribute, and it poses no threat. It also conveys confidence and this is an important, subconscious turn-on for everyone.

✳ **Femininity:** Most guys are turned on to feminine girls. Dressing fashionably in short skirts, tasteful jewelry, and stylish heels will turn most heads. Long hair is also a popular turn on for many red-blooded American males. (Think Barbie)

✳ **Happy smilers:** Guys love it when a girl smiles a lot. It makes her very approachable and enjoyable to talk to.

* **Good morals:** This is a definite turn-on for the "Right Guy." But if a guy is looking for a one night stand, he will pass you by as fast as he can say . . . next!

* **Have your act together:** Everyone is impressed with a person who has his or her act together (examples: good job, ambition, good appearance, politeness, social skills, and intelligence). These are all turn-ons for a healthy person.

* **Interests / Talents:** Guys like it when you're really interested in something you have a passion for: Such as sports, cooking, music, or something they might also be interested in. Having an interest or hobby projects independence, and that's a turn on. So get out there and flaunt your interests & talents!

Turn-ons for Women

OK guys, here's the good or bad news, depending on who you are. Women are similar to guys in some ways. Most guys are very visual. So are women. Most guys are attracted to a woman's physique/hot body and so are women.

Here are my observations of what most women are attracted to:

* **Good looks:** If you have a good looking face, smile, nose, and jaw, girls will definitely check you out.

* **Hot body:** If you're a personal trainer or body builder with great chest, biceps, legs of iron, and six pack abs, you are in! Chicks will throw themselves in front of you. They subconsciously feel protected by this man of steel.

* **Tall:** If you are 6 ft. or over, girls will give you a chance. Girls love tall guys. It's a subconscious turn-on for them. They feel secure with this tall warrior.

✱ **Financial Security:** Women have a sense of security if you are a financially savvy man. They feel comforted by money in many ways. Financial security can attract certain types of women. Often they are _Gold Diggers_, but most women want a man with some sort of financial success. They see your finances as comfort for them.

✱ **Attitude:** Many women get attracted to men with a cocky, self-assured attitude. For some ridiculous reason, this "bad boy" persona turns girls on. Be observant, as this small red flag could hint towards insecurities. But many women love these men of attitude.

✱ **Confidence:** Chicks dig guys that exude confidence. Even if you're not the most confident guy in the world, you must at least try to fake it. Confidence is a huge turn-on for girls, it's a must! But don't overdo it, that can be a turn-off. Just remember, a confident man is a sexy man, and women love it!

✱ **Sense of Humor:** OK guys, get out your joke book because girls love to laugh. Girls feel comfortable when you make them laugh. It's a big turn-on for them and it makes them feel at ease. It's a way to break down their defense.

✱ **Popular:** If you're a popular guy of any kind, girls will be very attracted to you.
Some examples are:

- ✱TV personality
- ✱ Sports figure
- ✱ Politician
- ✱ Singer
- ✱ Movie actor
- ✱ Rock Star

✱ **Power position:** Women love guys who have a powerful position. It's another sense of security.
Some examples are:

- ✱ President of a bank
- ✱ CEO of a big company
- ✱ Owner of a very successful business, especially club owners
- ✱ Top man in his field
- ✱ A man of stature in his community

✸ **Intelligence:** Most women are intrigued by a man of intelligence, But often it must be the kind of intelligence that they can relate to. If your intellect is over their heads or not of their interest, it will probably bore them. So you must use your intelligence to figure out what turns them on. Example; witty humor is a definite turn-on and displays confidence.

✸ **Fashionable:** Women are typically attracted to men who are trendy and fashionable in nature.
Some examples are:

- ✸ Wears the latest fashions/shoes
- ✸ Possesses the latest electronic toys
  (example: cell phone, computer, stereo, TV, etc.)
- ✸ Drives the fanciest car
- ✸ Has chic décor in his apartment or house
- ✸ Reads the trendiest magazines
- ✸ Wears the latest hip hairstyle
- ✸ Wears expensive jewelry and watches
- ✸ Uses the latest lingo
- ✸ Wears cool sunglasses

✸ **Good Dancer:** Girls love guys who are good dancers! If you are a good dancer, girls will want to dance with you all night long, so sign up for a dance class and brush up on your salsa, swing, and hustle!

✸ **Ambition:** Most women are attracted to guys who have motivation and ambition. They like the feeling that they are with a guy who's a mover and shaker.

OK guys, I hope this gave you a few ideas on how to shape up. **Now get to work!**

Turn-offs for Women

✸ **Possessiveness:** Women are generally turned off by possessive and controlling guys. It displays immaturity and lack of confidence. Most women won't give you a chance if they sense this character trait in you. Unless you're great looking and rich!

* **Over confidence:** Being confident is very good! But over confident is a self-centered, egotistical attitude that women pick up on and they won't give you the time of day, unless you're a rock star.

* **Bad hygiene:** Ok guys let's go . . . Shave your back and trim those nose and ear hairs. Brush your teeth and hair. . . Do you have dandruff? Belly-button lint? Bad breath? Rotted and missing teeth? Maybe mommy should give you a bath and put on a fresh diaper before your next date.

* **Unemployed:** Get a job! Get off your lazy ass and do something! Women hate unemployed guys! I know sometimes things can be tough, but start mowing lawns or shoveling driveways, if you want a date. Girls respect guys who bring in the dough, it's as simple as that!

* **Extremely overweight or underweight:** Take a good look at yourself. If you were a woman, would you want to date you? If you are too fat or too skinny, get it together, because being too overweight or underweight is a physical turn-off for most women.

* **Laziness:** It's time to get off the couch and take out the garbage, because chicks are definitely turned off by laziness. Maybe you should try some ginseng!

* **Checking out other chicks:** This is a big turn-off. Do not check out other girls when on a date! Girls will cross you off their list so fast that you won't even remember you went on a date. Keep your eyes in your sockets and on your date or stay single.

* **Indecisiveness:** Women are definitely turned off to guys who can't make a definite decision. This displays a lack of mental strength and confidence. Thus, making the women feel subconsciously unprotected. When most women sense a guy's indecisive nature, she'll be outta there faster then she can say WIMP!

* **Tight Wad:** Girls hate cheap guys! Sometimes you just gotta breakdown and spend a few bucks to impress your date. You don't have to over do it and be a big spender, but don't be a cheap tight wad! Girls love it when you show them a great time and make it a date worth remembering. You'll be glad you did!

* **Bad Manners:** Where did you learn your manners? . . . . . . At the zoo?

Keep these hints in mind when on a date:

* Don't chew with your mouth open and spit food all over your date
* Don't belch like a pig, especially in public
* Don't fart in a movie theatre, during dinner or while having sex
* Don't scratch your privates in public and in front of her
* Don't get stupid, loud, drunk, and puke on her . . .
  It could ruin your date!

Relationship Type

Roommate Marriages

What's up with this? These are the types of marriages we're seeing a lot of these days. Are they really in love or are they just married because they were roommates first and then they figured, Well I guess we're in love because we've known each other for a few years in college and we were roommates for a while, we both have the same friends, so I guess I love him? This is by far the most ridiculous idea of love in this decade. I see it all the time. I don't think these girls and guys have any idea what love is, partially because they're not raised in a love expressive family. So how can they know what love is? Couples are falling in friendship, not falling in love. You must have both. Roommate marriages are marriages of convenience not love. Roommate marriages are the most shallow of marriages: You go your way, and I'll go mine and we'll meet in bed when we go to sleep. You go out with your buddies, and I'll go out with the girls and maybe we'll meet up. What happened to real marriages? Marriages where two people who are best friends also love, honor and cherish each other, share common goals and are willing to work together through the ups and downs. **What happened to these marriages?** Or are most marriages these days becoming roommate marriages?

Bitter Stories

"These are just a few of the true stories that made me the BITTER MAN I am today."

"Mercedes"

Now here's a good situation to meet a nice girl. Everyone says that you should go to church functions to meet the kind of girl you want. And I did, and have, many times but had no luck meeting anyone I had a connection with. But I went to this really great church that I attend from time to time.

They had a Salsa dance lesson on Friday night at 6:00 p.m. (I had taken about 2 years of private lessons so I'd feel confident when dancing with a girl as well as impress her and get a date with someone special.) So here I am in this nice church atmosphere with about 50 men and women taking the Salsa class, when I see this very cute Latin girl. As we took turns changing partners, I finally had her as my partner and we began dancing and talking and seemed to have a bit of an attraction towards each other. So at the end of the class we exchanged phone numbers and I mentioned to her that I enjoyed dancing with her and that if she needed someone to practice dancing with, I have a bit of experience and could show her a few steps. She smiled and said "maybe I'll see you next week." We then went on our merry ways and I hoped I'd see her again next Friday. The next day the phone rings . . . and guess who it was? It was Mercedes calling me, can you believe it? The girl I was so attracted to was calling me! Usually it's the girls I don't want to call me that call, but this was a great feeling! Anyway, she asked me if I wanted to get together and go out. I was in shock! But I remained cool, calm and collected and said "Sure, when is good for you?" She said, "How about tomorrow night?" I said, "That's fine with me." So we hung up after a short and nice conversation, and I anticipated tomorrow night. So now it's Sunday night. She came over on time in her cute red convertible and we went out to dinner, Salsa dancing, walked, talked, laughed and had a great time. When we got back to my place, I gave her a hug and said "I had a great time; let's get together soon." We both agreed, and that was the end of a perfect night and date.

The next week came and she called me and left a message

on my voice mail to say hi. I called her back and we talked a bit and then I asked her if she'd like to go ice skating. She said, "Sure, that would be fun!" We went out again and had dinner and went ice skating at this great indoor arena. It was another great date! We really had a lot of fun talking and getting to know each other deeper and with respect. She was a courtroom stenographer and seemed to enjoy her job and I respected that. Anyway, it was another perfect night ending with a hug and a kiss on the cheek to keep things comfortable.

As the days went on, we would call each other and go out for lunch. Our friendship was getting closer by the week. I was getting excited, but I didn't want to rush things and scare her off. I continued to ask her out, and we continued to have a great time. Now we were friends for about a month and a half. I was looking forward to seeing her this evening when she called me and said, "Hi Antone! What's new? I just called because I want to tell you something very exciting that happened to me." I said, "really? tell me about it!" She said, "I just went on a date with this really nice guy and I want to ask you how I should handle it? I really like him!" Right there I almost got sick! I was feeling nauseated! Physically and mentally I was boiling! I was trying to stay cool. So I asked. . . "Can I ask you a question? Why was it that he was a date? Was I a date?" She replied, "Oh, I'm sorry, I thought we we friends." I said, "Yes we are friends but I'm also very attracted to you, and it's too hard for me to be just friends." "Maybe we should just stop being friends because it's a bit confusing for me, even though it's been real nice going out with you," She then replied in a cool tone voice, "Ok, Take care, Bye." I was deeply hurt & disgusted! I never heard from her again. I tried calling her a few weeks later but her phone was disconnected and she had moved.

And thus THE BITTER MAN was born!

So what did I learn from this? Well, as I think back on this short friendship, I feel that she turned out to be a USER. She was nice, but a nice USER. So my advice to you is don't let someone take advantage of you. I went too long without noticing this flaw in her character. I should have detected it sooner. I should've found out what she wanted in a relationship and told her what I was looking for in a girl. I was too nice to her and shouldn't have let myself get in the "FRIEND ZONE."

"Laura"

Here's a girl who I met at a Halloween party. We were introduced by a mutual friend and we began talking and hitting it off. She was very attractive and sweet, and I was definitely interested. But the only catch was . . . she had a boyfriend. (As most attractive girls do) But as we were conversing she mentioned to me that her relationship wasn't going in the direction she wanted it to. She wanted a more stable, affectionate guy, and she didn't feel the same way about him as she used to. So I was taking this as a subtle hint that she might be interested in getting to know me better.

I was a bit excited, but once again stayed cool, calm and friendly. So as time went on, we became friends - going out for dinner, shopping and having a great time. I also had in the back of my mind, "If it eventually doesn't work out with her boyfriend, I'll be next in line." (I wasn't the Bitter Man I am today) So I kept on going out with her, hoping that she'd break up with him soon and then I'd have a good shot at dating her. But, once again, I didn't push too hard as to scare her away; I remained a good friend to her. She wan't a USER because she would buy me small presents, offer to pay for dinner half of the time, and we did favors for each other. She was a giving person who had a good job, and I respected that. Our friendship was growing stronger and I was getting more attracted to her by the day; and I felt she was really liking me more as well. It had become a real nice friendship! We remained friends for about a year but never got romantic other than a hug and a quick kiss goodbye, because her boyfriend was still in the picture. (Even though he still wasn't giving her what she wanted) I did, however, show her a lot of attention and interest in a gentlemanly way. Then one day she called me and said, "Antone, let's get together - things are not working out with my boyfriend, and I want to tell you about it." I said, "Sure, I'll pick you up and we'll go to dinner and talk about it." She said, "Great! I'll be ready in an hour." So now we're at a nice restaurant and she begins to tell me that she broke up with her boyfriend last week, and how sweet I am.

(Now I'm getting excited - like a dog about to get a bone.) But no, not for MR. NICE GUY ANTONE! She then begins to tell me "I met this guy at a concert last week and we really hit it off. I've been seeing him a lot this week and I think he's "THE ONE." He drives a Harley and owns his own motorcycle business . . . and guess what? I'm going to move in with him next week! Isn't that exciting? Aren't you happy for me??!!" I just about vomited on the table! I was sick to my stomach and sinking in my chair. I then stated my claim. I said, "Look, I've been going out with you for about a year, and we have a great time together. I am really attracted to you but didn't want to make any romantic advances towards you because you had a boyfriend. I just figured it would be common sense that if it didn't work out with him, you'd date me!"

"Now, you meet a guy you hardly know, you THINK you're in love and you're going to move in with him! What are you, nuts?!!!!" She then states, "But he's really good looking and has his own motorcycle business." I said, "I'm really attracted to you and I want to date you, but I can't just be "friends". If you're not interested in me then we shouldn't go out anymore." In an upset voice, she said, "I can't believe it! OK, if that's how you feel! Take Care!!"

We both got up, went home, and I never heard from her again. **Another typical ending to a BITTER MAN'S story!**

What have I learned from this? I spent way too much time hanging out with her! Many of my married friends tell me that they were friends for a long time before they got serious. So that's why I've been giving our friendship a chance. But never again! I've lost my patience! If I don't feel a connection in a few dates, I'm outta there! She was most likely a GOLD DIGGER looking for financial security with Motorcycle Man and didn't see it with me. Oh well . . . NEXT!

"Sophenia"

This is a girl who I met while I was meeting with a client at his office. She was the receptionist, and her name is Sophenia. When I walked in, I said hello to her and we talked casually for a few minutes. I thought she was very nice, as well as attractive. I then saw my client and did my business. On the way out I spoke with Sophenia briefly again and said, "It was nice meeting you. Have a great day!" I thought to myself that we seemed to have a connection but I wasn't sure . . . anyway, I'll see her again next week and possibly ask her to lunch.

I then went home around 5:00 pm and, as soon as I get in the door, the phone rings. Guess who? That's right! It was Sophenia. How did she get my number? What could she want? That was pretty gutsy of her to call a guy that she just met for a few minutes. But I loved it! She said hi and didn't give me a serious reason why she called just that she wanted to chat. (Correct me if I'm wrong but I think this is a hint she's interested) Anyway I told her I was hungry and would she like to go grab a bite to eat? She said sure! So we met and had a few slices of pizza and even went for a short bike ride around the local lake. It was great! We really seemed to hit it off. Then as time went on we went out a few times and when I tried to kiss her . . . Guess what? She said . . . "Oh didn't I tell you? I have a boyfriend!" So I just sucked it up and moved on. Now months have passed and from time to time she calls explaining to me how her boyfriend doesn't treat her well and they argue all the time. I listen to her plight patiently. Then again and again she would call me month after month, year after year whining to me about her other boyfriends who don't treat her right. Every time she called I thought it was her way of hinting to me to ask her out. But she would say, "no, I can't go out with you because I'm in a relationship and he wouldn't like that." Then one night she called me again to tell me her woes. I then said to her firmly, "Look, you obviously have a problem! Why do you keep calling me to tell me that your boyfriends treat you like s#!t!!? You have a problem if you keep getting into relationships with these types of guys and stay with them. I would treat you like a princess and you wouldn't have these problems if you dated me, but you're not interested in me. You keep looking for trouble! You're sick and you need help!" That's exactly what I said. I then asked, "Why is it that you're not interested in me??!!" She said, "I like tall guys." I said, "well let me see . . . you're 5 ft. tall and I'm 5'8", how much taller do you need?" She replies, "Oh, my boyfriend is 6ft 5in." Oh yeah girl you're a winner! So go back to your tall respectful relationship and don't call me anymore! See Ya! Click................................

So what have I learned from her? She was a CONFUSED CHICK not knowing what she wanted. Till this day she still calls me and says she hates men and can't find a good guy! The good thing is that I didn't spend too much time going out with her . . . THANK GOD! . . I'm learning!

"Jill"

Well here is a different way of meeting someone. Here I am sitting on the bench at my local car wash waiting for my car to go through the system. When out of the blue, this conservatively dressed, attractive girl sits next to me and is waiting for her car as well. I thought to myself, "I must at least try to start a conversation with her." But before I did, I glanced at her left hand to make sure I didn't see a ring on her finger . . . Then I said to myself, "what the hell, I have 5 minutes to make a move!" So I said, "hello" and we introduced ourselves to each other. "Hi, I'm Antone - nice to meet you. What's your name?"
"Jill" she replied. Then we made some small talk, and I asked her what she did for a living. She said she worked as an accountant's assistant and was also a part-time model. I mentioned that I work with a lot of photographers and might be able to get her some work. I gave her my card and said, "Give me a call when you get a chance and I'll give you some numbers of people I know who might be able to direct some modeling work your way." She said, "thanks!" And then our cars were ready and off we went - back to reality. I never

thought I'd see or hear from her again.

About a week passed and, yep, you guessed it! The phone rings and it's Jill! We talked on the phone for a while about her modeling work and basic conversation; and then I asked her out to lunch, and she said, "sure!" This was the beginning to another one of my "FRIENDSHIPS". I can't believe I keep doing this! Anyway, the first thing I asked was, "Do you have a boyfriend?" She said, "yes, I'm living with him." I figured ok this is going nowhere, but I guess I'll be friends with her, you never know where it'll lead. And so, it was another 2 year friendship to add to my collection of girl "FRIENDS". As time went on, we went to lunches and dinners and all the things that friends do. I thought she was HOT but I knew there was nothing I could do since she had a boyfriend. She then started telling me that her boyfriend wan't paying much attention to her or spending any quality time with her. So I was patient and supportive . . . even though I just wanted to kiss her. (That's the romantic side of me.)

Then the next day we went out to dinner to celebrate her new job as an accountant. I bought her a congratulatory present and we had a great night. She began to tell me that her and her boyfriend were breaking up because he didn't want to marry her. (I thought to myself this guy's a jerk - he doesn't know what he's got! Jill's amazing!) She didn't seem upset by the break-up because I guess she was over it. I then thought to myself, "this is my chance to let her know how I feel." So here I go again . . . As we were enjoying our desserts I said, "Jill, I want you to know I think you're fantastic and beautiful! I know this is crazy but I really care about you and would love to date you. How do you feel?" She said, "Antone I've known you too long - I can't date you, even though I have romantic feelings toward you." I said, "What is that supposed to mean? You've known me too long and have romantic feelings towards me?" She said, "I just like you as a friend." I said, "But you said you have romantic feelings towards me." She just looked at me and smiled. Needless to say, I was frustrated. So I paid the bill and drive her home. We never talked after that night.

So what have I learned from that? I'm STUPID! That's what! I keep believing in this fantasy of love. That this nice girl is going to see that I'm her knight in shining armor. Instead, I'm her "FRIEND" in shining armor and I wind up getting frustrated. I asked for it! I have no one to blame but myself! So don't make the same mistakes I made. Don't be such a nice "FRIEND"!

"Koral"

This is a girl I met while I was playing drums with a band at an outdoor jazz festival. Her name is Koral, and she was working at a local radio station's advertising booth at the festival. On my break I was at the booth greeting local fans and Koral was there as well. I introduced myself and we began conversing about music and traveling. She mentioned that she was from Nicaragua but she had lived in the states most of her life. She was a very pretty Latin girl and was dressed very sharp. I was very attracted to her appearance and personality. We talked about Costa Rica because I just got back from vacation there and she also liked to travel. She also worked at an airline company so she traveled a lot. Anyway, we talked for a while and then I had to go back to the stage. I did feel a connection between us but didn't want to be too forward and ask for her number since I had just met her. So the next day I called a friend of Koral's who works with her who I knew a bit. I left a message on her voice mail saying something to this effect; "Hi this is Antone . . . I had met your friend Koral yesterday and it was nice talking with her, I was interested in meeting her again, could you pass this message and my number on to her? Thanks!" Not really thinking that she would call . . . but a few hours later guess what? That's right! The phone rings and it's Koral. Wow how nice! We talked for about an hour and I made her laugh a lot! We really seemed to hit it off over the phone and I was feeling confident that she would at least go on a date with me. I asked her to lunch and she said yes, we went and had a nice afternoon. We then went out a few times after that and always laughed a lot (we had laughing in common I guess). At the end of each date I tried to kiss her but she just gave me a quick kiss and off she went. I guess that was my hint that she didn't seem too interested in me. Oh well, I've been through it many times before! So I guess I won't pursue her because it didn't seem to be going anywhere. But we had one more planned date next weekend. We got together on Friday night and went to a friend's party. We sat and talked a bit and then I put a little pressure on her to tell me her story - Was she interested, or not? I'm not going to spend a year being "FRIENDS" so she can tell me that she met some guy and is going to move in with him (refer to other Bitter Stories). I told her through our relaxed party conversation that I was interested in getting to know her better and was looking for a more serious relationship. I asked her how she felt. She then said, "You're a real nice guy" (you know you're doomed when you hear the "NICE GUY" words) but I met this guy in Amsterdam, and I'm really attracted to him; but, we don't get along very well and we argue a lot." "But I really think he's great and I think I can change him, so I'm going back to visit him next week - he may be "THE ONE!" I just about dropped my drink on the floor and thought to myself this girl is f*#!ing nuts! Listen to what she's saying . . . She's going all the way to Amsterdam to be with a guy who treats her like crap and probably just wants a piece of ass! Is this the kind of girl I want? Absolutely not! I'm outta here!

So what's the lesson here? Well I got out fast. Just a few dates and I saw the writing on the wall. She was definitely a CONFUSED CHICK! She wanted a guy who was half way around the world, who mentally abused her, and whom she thought she could change. Yeah right! WHATEVER! See ya!

"Jesanna"

Here is another interesting story. I went to Costa Rica for a 10 day vacation. I left on Valentine's Day as to tempt romantic luck. Did it work? Well . . . ? Let me tell you that I did have a wonderful vacation. And on the last day I was sitting on a bench in front of the hotel waiting for the bus to take me back to the airport, when this cute Costa Rican girl (Jesanna) sits next to me. I said, "Hello" and we started to chat - though her English was broken. I could tell that she was a very sweet and friendly person, as many Costa Ricans are. Anyway, we talked for about 15 minutes and then exchanged numbers and addresses and said goodbye. The bus then came and off I went to the airport. On the day I arrived home, and started getting back to my routine, lo and behold guess who calls? You got it! Jesanna! Oh my God! I couldn't believe it. She came from a lower income family. I was surprised she could afford the long distance call. So now this began a 3 month long distance relationship. We were writing letters, sending photos, e-mailing, faxing and calling. We laughed, talked and got to know each other very well. It was fun! She made it perfectly clear that she wanted to see me again ASAP. In the back of my mind I'm thinking . . . WARNING   : RICH AMERICAN GREEN CARD TRAP. I offered for her to visit with me, but she couldn't due to money, work, school and visa/passport complications. So I told her that maybe I would visit in the fall. She said that was such a long time away, couldn't I visit sooner? I said, "Maybe, let's see how our long distance friendship progresses." So we continued contacting each other another month and then I broke down and decided to go back to Costa Rica. Call me nuts, but I'm looking for someone special and I felt that she may be the one. So I arranged a flight and off I went chasing my fantasy of love.

So this is it! I fly to San Jose and I'm going through immigration, looking for her in the crowd of hundreds in the arrival area. There she was looking for me, and we hugged and both felt a little strange, but excited. We then went to her house. It was a very small poor looking home with holes in the ceiling and a 1960s black and white TV. It was something I wasn't used to. She came from a poor family with 6 children and a few dogs and cats - just like in a movie. I felt like I was in a Discovery documentary. Anyway, her family, cousins and friends came to see me, and they all were so very warm, friendly, happy, simple, poor people. So for a week I spent time with her and her family. We all went out dancing and spent time getting to know each other. Jesanna was so smart and sweet, and I was really falling for her, but hadn't tried to kiss her yet. So here goes . . . We went for a walk together in her town and held hands and then I tried to kiss her. She jumped back and said, "What are you doing?" "This must not happen again!" I was shocked!! What's wrong with a little kiss? I come all the way from Florida, we become friends and I can't even get a kiss? What's up with this????????!!!!!! I guess she comes from a different culture and is very old fashioned. I guess I need to be married to her before I can kiss her. OK, I guess this is not for me! So I continued spending two more days there with her and her family. I had a serious talk with her, and I told her I'd like her to visit me and spend some time with me if she was interested. I then gave her a kiss in the cheek and off I went back home to Florida. Within a week I received a letter from her:

Dear Antone,
  You are a very special person but I can't continue our friendship. A long distance relationship is too complicated for us and I must finish out my studies and help my family. Thank you for everything.

Love,
Jesanna

Ok what have we learned from this? Long distance relationships and different cultures are very difficult to deal with! It was a nice experience getting close to another family and culture. But it was also heart breaking and frustrating! I, myself, won't go to another country and try to fall in love.

"April"

Here's a short story about a girl whom I was set up with. My friend's mom knew a girl who really wanted to meet a guy for a serious, meaningful relationship. So the first thing I asked was, is she cute? My friend's mom said, "Oh yes! And she's a dance teacher - 28 years old." So I figured how bad could she be? She's a good age, and dancers are usually fit. Plus my friend's mom said she's smart and is a great person. So I figured what the hell? I'll give her a call. So I did, and we had a nice conversation. I asked her to send me a photo of herself, since she lived about an hour away from me, but she said she didn't have one. (WARNING: If a person doesn't want to send you a photo of themself this could be a sign they aren't the prettiest rose in the bunch!) But she said, "Why don't you visit me tonight and we can go out to dinner after I teach my dance class." I said, "That's fine, I'll meet you at 7:00pm tonight." So I took a shower, got dressed and took a drive out to redneckville, where she lived. I am now looking for the dance studio where she teaches . . . and I find it! But it winds up being a huge tin warehouse with pickup trucks and 4-wheelers parked everywhere. I then got out of my car and walked through the dirt parking lot and mud puddles and found my way in. Now, I have no clue what to expect . . . Could she be a hot country girl like in the calendars? Hmmmm. . . . maybe?!! So I looked to my left and I saw a country line dance class being taught by some cowboy dude. Then I looked to my right and saw a clogging dance class being taught by a girl named April. That was her! Oh my GOD!!! She was unbelievable! She was about 4 feet tall, about 175 pounds with short curly hair, freckles, braces and she was wearing a plaid mini-skirt with sneakers. I wish I had a camera! She was straight out of a comedy show! I just walked out quietly, got in my car and took off! Some may say I'm shallow, but she wasn't quite my type.

So what have I learned from this experience? Never to be set up with a girl unless you see her photo first. And I've also learned why they call them blind dates . . . Because you wish you were blind when you meet them!

"Nicolette"

This is a short story about a girl whom I met through some ballroom dance friends. Her father owned the studio where I took lessons. All of the teachers and students went out one night to a restaurant and I was introduced to Nicolette. She was a very nice attractive girl who was a professional nail technician and was also studying for her real estate license.

We spoke for a while and had a few drinks and laughs. At the end of the night I asked her if she'd like to go out sometime. She said, "sure", and gave me her business card. The following week I gave her a call, and we made plans to go to dinner and a movie. When we went out we had a nice time! She was a very happy and fun person and always smiled. I really liked her! We went out about three times within a month. I then called her for the fourth date but I felt this standoffish feeling. We spoke for a while and I asked her why she hadn't called me lately. She said she didn't want to give me any false hope.

I asked her if there was a problem between us. She said, You are a very nice guy and a great catch! But I just don't feel anything for you. I'm sorry. I tried, but I'm being honest. I need to have some kind of feeling and I'm not having it with you." I said, "I understand" and thanked her for her honesty.

At least she told me truly how she felt about me. I felt she was sincere, and she didn't give me some crazy excuse or ignore me. Nicolette was the only girl who had the respect to be honest and truthful to me. We remain friends to this day. What's the lesson to be learned? Hmmmm, well, I really respect a girl who is honest with me, even if it hurts a bit - it's better than playing games and being lied to. Nicolette is a very classy girl because she respects herself and others. Too bad it didn't work out.

"Alexis"

OK, get ready for the ride of your life! This one takes the cake! Everyone says, "Why don't you try the personal ads?" Well, I've tried them quite a few times but with no luck. So I figured I like Costa Rica - I've been there twice. Maybe I should put an ad in a Costa Rican newspaper and see what happens. And so I did. Well guess what? I received a few letters from girls I wasn't interested in; but one called me and spoke perfect English. It was interesting to say the least. She worked at a company and had the use of a computer. So she e-mailed me a photo of herself, and I was impressed. We then began a correspondence through e-mails and phone calls. She seemed sweet and funny and everything I wanted in a personality. I didn't want to go to Costa Rica because I wanted her to visit me and see my life style. She wanted to visit me but couldn't afford a ticket. I said I'm not rich but I'd buy her a ticket to visit me. She was excited! And so was I! After about six months of e-mailing and calling, we set a date for her to visit.

Now, today is the day she arrives. I go to the airport to pick her up and wait for her at the gate, I was a bit nervous and I was thinking. . . . What if we're not attracted to each other? Oh well, I guess I can chalk it up to another crazy experience and we can be friends.

Well, here she comes out of the gate . . . we see each other and I give her a big hug but her hug was loose. I said, "It's so nice to finally see you in person! You're beautiful!" She just said, "Thank You," and was quiet. I sensed something strange. Maybe she was just tired from traveling. I was a bit confused. Maybe she wasn't attracted to me. This was not the anticipated beginning I thought it would be. I then got her baggage, and as we drove to my house, she didn't say much. Maybe she was nervous? Oh well, I'll just make her comfortable at my house. When we got back to my house she said she didn't feel well so she took a nap on the couch. (Refer to *Sickly Chick* CD) Now I'm feeling strange - we just met and there's no vibe at all!! What happened to the six months of excitement on the phone and in the e-mails? Maybe she's just nervous and shy?

I'm thinking she'll warm up once she gets to know me. When she woke up, I said, "Let's go to dinner at my favorite Italian restaurant." When we got there, she didn't seem impressed. We then got home and she said she was tired, and we went to sleep early in separate rooms. OK, this is beginning to feel strange, but tomorrow is another day. The next day came and I took her to lunch and she didn't seem impressed and didn't even say thank you for anything. Now I'm starting to think something is very wrong here. She just watches TV, doesn't wash the dishes after she eats, doesn't seem to like anything so far, and is definitely not interested in me. Now I still have to be nice to my guest for a few more days, even if we don't hit it off. So I'll be a gentleman and see this situation through until she leaves.

Now today is Friday and I'm playing drums with a good jazz-reggae-pop band at Cafe Tu Tu Tango - a fun and exciting tourist restaurant. I had arranged a table with some friends for her to sit at. I told her to order whatever she wanted. I then went to play drums for 45 minutes and when I got back to sit with her she was exchanging numbers with a guy I didn't even know. Now I'm fuming! I thought to myself . . . What the hell is this all about? Am I being used??!!! I thought that was very inconsiderate, but I kept my cool. On the way home, I asked her why she was exchanging numbers with that guy? She said he offered her a job in Miami. (Yeah right!) I didn't buy it! I told her that I didn't feel that was very considerate of her. It made for an uncomfortable rest of the night.

The next day I asked her how she felt about the situation of visiting me. Did she want to stay or leave - because she didn't seem to be happy. She said she wanted to stay and get to know me better. So I said, "OK, let's forget about our little tiff and move on." So we spent the day driving around, and I showed her the local Orlando sites. In the evening I had to play drums at Cafe Tu Tu Tango again, so she came with me. Just before I was about to go on stage, she asked me for the keys to the car. I said, "why?" She said because she wanted to sleep in it. And she did, all night long. While I was playing drums, she was sleeping in my car, I couldn't believe it! Why couldn't she enjoy the music, dancing, atmosphere and my friends? Instead, she chose to sleep in the car on a Saturday night on a free vacation to Orlando, Florida with a guy that was treating her like a princess! I did everything I could to make her happy and comfortable, but she was a miserable person! So that night came to an end. I figured that I have two more days and then she's outta here! But I still wanted to be a courteous host. The next day came, and she promised to make me a traditional Costa Rican dinner. So we went to the supermarket and she asked me what I wanted to have? I was so happy that I would get a home cooked dinner. I said, "Anything you like is fine with me." After all, being a single guy, any home cooked meal is great to me! But she didn't seem enthusiastic about making dinner. She picked up some meat and dropped it down a few times almost like she didn't care . . . in a lazy fashion. She then looked at me and said, "You know I really don't feel like cooking dinner for you." "Why don't you get some frozen food?" Now my blood was boiling! This girl couldn't do anything for me. Not compliment me, thank me, help me with anything or at least be friendly to me. Nothing!! She was just a miserable person! I just looked at her and said. "Well if you don't feel like making dinner for us, then I don't want you in my house any longer! In fact, I want you out right now, you SELF-CENTERED USER!!!!" I drove her back to my house real fast! And she said, "I need to use your phone." I said, "The only phone call you can make is for the taxi to pick you up and get you out of my house." I called the taxi, and it was the longest 20 minutes of my life. She was supposed to leave tomorrow morning, but she was being thrown out now! She said, "I don't have any money, a credit card or cell phone." I said, "How stupid are you to travel to another country and to a guys house that you don't even know? Then you treat me with total disrespect and you don't even bring a credit card or any money! If you would have been at least a courteous guest, you wouldn't be in this predicament right now. But I've taken way too much disrespect from you and you've got to go!" The taxi pulled up and I threw her luggage in the trunk.

I gave her $20.00 cash and $10.00 in quarters for the phone. I said, "I'm sorry you put yourself in this position, but don't ever call me again!" I slammed the taxi door shut and off she went! I was very upset that I had to do that but enough is enough! She had a flight to leave the next morning. Maybe she'll think of how she treated me when she slept at the airport.

So what did I learn from this? Don't ever let anyone take advantage of you like this. I let it go on too long. She was a total USER looking for a free ticket to the states and I fell for it! I've learned a big lesson, and I'll never forget this experience! And these are just a few of the stories that made me "THE BITTER MAN!"

The Bitter End

Thanks again for reading my book. I hope you enjoyed it, and I hope you learned something. I'd just like to share some remaining thoughts with you before I go.

I found out that people are who they are and you should never expect them to change, but rather accept and appreciate them as they are. It's your choice to decide who you spend your time with. **Don't try to change anyone!** Love, honor and respect your mate, and have at least 75% good times in a relationship. If you are not getting what you want, get out - or you're in for a long ride. Be aware of who you are dating. Look for the clear, early signs of incompatibility. You don't need to spend months getting to know if you're compatible with someone. Just learn to be aware of the personalities that are compatible with yours, The best relationships flow naturally. And don't forget, be careful dating out there, it can be **BITTER!**

- End -

www.thebitterman.com

A. Christopher
aka **Mr. Bitterman**